Measuring Business Intelligence Success

A Business Intelligence Capability Maturity Model

Dorothy Miller

DM **M**ORRISEY

Published by D M Morrisey & Associates

Library of Congress Cataloging-in-Publication data:
Miller, Dorothy.
      Measuring Business Intelligence Success
      D M Morrisey
      SAN   8 5 3 – 3 7 4 1
      ISBN 978-0-9794146-3-3
          1. Data warehousing. 2. Business Intelligence

Printed in United States of America

For more information on <u>Measuring Business Intelligence Success,</u> check the author's web site at www.Redstone360.com

10 9 8 7 6 5 4 3 2 1

CONTENTS

CONTENTS

CONTENTS

CONTENTS

ACKNOWLEDGEMENTS

Thanks to all my friends and family for their continuing support and understanding. Thanks especially to my daughters, Stephanie and Shannon, and my granddaughters, Ariel and Dawn - for being there for me. Skip Davis has provided some key assistance in completing the manuscript. During the writing of this book a good friend died. I would like to acknowledge and thank Dale Graves for his friendship of over 15 years.

INTRODUCTION

Chapter Contents
1. Objectives of the Book
2. What is Business Intelligence
3. Auditing Business Intelligence Assets
4. The Business Intelligence Capability Maturity Model
5. Using the Audit Results

1. Objectives of the book

Business Intelligence assets are crucial to the success of an organization. Audit and assessment of the Business Intelligence assets have become increasingly urgent. Most organizations do not even know what those assets are. Someone says they need new business information. Another Business Intelligence application is designed and built. The library of information in the Data Warehouse is expanded. Either the new Business Intelligence application doesn't work and issues like data accuracy and integration problems kill the project (and many of the people associated with it.) Or, it does work. The systems or better business information, faster (or not) and things go on. Everyone assumes things are better. And, generally they are.

Should we just accept that people are getting the Business Intelligence that they need? What kind of expenditures, in money, time and other resources, have we spent on Business Intelligence? For many organizations, this can be literally millions of dollars. How do we identify and clarify where and how well our resources are being spent? How do we know what risks we are facing? Those risks could be internal to the systems, as well as, opportunities lost because of failures to supply the required Business Intelligence to management and operations staff.

The objectives of this book are to:

· provide a strong rationale for the audit of Business Intelligence, i.e. identify and clarify the reasons for auditing and assessing the Business Intelligence assets for an organization; and

· provide a framework, guide, and set of tools for a Business Intelligence audit.

Incentive and Rationale for Business Intelligence Audit. There is currently no industry guide and no set of practices and protocols for auditing of Business Intelligence Assets. Because of the pressing needs for Business Intelligence, there has been little time for an organization to sideline resources into such an audit. One of the goals of this book is to provide a strong incentive to organization management to place a high priority on the Business Intelligence audit.

In order to achieve this, management requires a clear 'best practices' Guide for the Business Intelligence Audit. We have selected the Capability Maturity Model as a foundation for this Business Intelligence Guide. This new TBIA Business Intelligence Capability Maturity Model® has been designed to provide a comprehensive guide to an audit of Business Intelligence Assets for the organization. This includes:

- What to measure, i.e. audit
- What are the Measurement Factors, i.e. Key Performance Indicators
- A scale or ruler for measurement
- How to Audit - i.e. an audit methodology, and
- How to use the audit results for improvement.

In this book, we will define, describe, and provide the necessary details and tell you how to use this Business Intelligence Capability Maturity Model. We will also take the final step in the Business Intelligence audit process and describe how to improve in the creation and management of Business Intelligence.

2. What is Business Intelligence

Organizations use Business Intelligence to monitor, report on, analyze and improve the performance of their business operations. The Business Intelligence systems include the complex spider web of architectures, infrastructures and engines which provide the capabilities to gather data, integrate it, and translate that data into a uniform 'single source of truth', i.e. quality business information. These people and systems use the information to manage and improve the business.

The raw data for Business Intelligence comes primarily from such sources as operational, i.e. transaction systems, legacy systems, and external sources.

The volume of data for most organizations has been increasing exponentially - and it is not unusual now to find those which face the daunting task of making sense of truly massive amounts of raw data. Fifty or more terrabytes of Data Warehouse storage are not unusual in today's Business Intelligence arena. Business Intelligence is the information product derived from sifting through the massive amounts of raw data available within an organization. Business Intelligence is also the infrastructures, methods, standards, processes and everything else involved in the collection, translation and integration, presentation and access of this product - i.e. everything involved in distilling the raw data into actionable information. For our purposes, we consider that all the data and infrastructures which are not specific to transaction or operational applications are part of the Business Intelligence Asset Base.

The raw data of the organization - i.e. from operations, external sources, legacy systems, - is collected, cleansed, integrated, translated and unified into a 'single source of truth'. Business Intelligence includes a library of business information which can be easily accessed by anyone in the organization. This library, the interfaces to the library and all the processes and structures involved in creating and using it - are part of the Business Intelligence Asset Base. If the industry evolves as anticipated - then this library of information will contain both structured data and unstructured data. It will be searchable, using tools and methods similar to the best available on the internet. And, the information may be real time, or close to real time.

The user interface and forms of business intelligence reporting have been varied. Spreadsheets have historically been the delivery format. The query and reporting tools are available and rapidly improving. We use on-line analytical processing (OLAP) and multi-dimensional data marts, dashboards, scorecards for cross organization tracking and management and excellent tools for statistical research into the data (i.e. Data Mining), forecasting and simulation, The reams of formerly unusable data can now be aggregated, segmented (`sliced and diced' is the industry slang) and analyzed in multiple ways, using a myriad of Business Intelligence tools.

3. Auditing Business Intelligence Assets

What is a Business Intelligence Audit

An Audit of the Business Intelligence Assets is a planned, formal review and assessment of the creation and management of Business Intelligence for the organization. An audit provides management a means to better understand the organization Business Intelligence assets. It is an organized, well defined method to identify and assess those assets and rate them against current industry standards. An Audit will include follow-up study of results, communication of those results and a planned program for using the results.

A Business Intelligence Audit requires

1. a clear identification and definition of Business Intelligence assets - i.e. what needs to be audited.
2. a rating system - i.e. how to measure
3. a measurement standard, i.e. scale for measurement
4. a well defined map to drive the audit process.

Why Audit Business Intelligence?

Business Intelligence operations are capital and resource intensive, requiring high investment in dollars and other tightly held resources. If successful and effective, the Business Intelligence Asset Base for an organization can produce extremely high returns. However, there are also too many examples of millions of dollars sunk with little or questionable return to the organization. There is no question that Business Intelligence systems can be a money and resources sponge. When the systems fail, the effects can be crippling. The industry has come through years of pain in the 'learn and suffer' trials. Now we have reached an industry experience level which should be providing a great percentage of the expected returns in terms of value to an organization. The Business Intelligence Asset Base for an organization should be giving a definite measurable boost to management decision making capabilities. However, many managers are wondering whether the returns are worth all the money which has been spent. Can we really see measurable value? There is no question that the concepts and capabilities of the Business Intelligence Assets are crucial for success for any business in today's world. When those assets are well designed, highly functional and integrated with the business requirements, then the business can and will see a dramatic return on investment dollars.

Most organizations need to improve on translating the chaos of enterprise data and making it available as information wherever and whenever needed, In order to improve, it is first necessary to identify what needs improvement. How does management evaluate the quality and effectiveness of all or any part of the Business Intelligence systems within an organization. The whole of the technology, basic infrastructures, the communications, interfaces and myriad other parts of the systems quite literally are part of and impact every part of the business structure and organization resources.

Some of the reasons for auditing Business Intelligence assets are to:

1. Determine how well the organization is doing in creating and managing Business Intelligence. An overall objective is to determine how well the organization is doing in creating and using Business Intelligence.

2. Understand the Business Intelligence assets. In most cases, no one in an organization really has a clear understanding of all the functions, structures, and even the related software which are part of the 'spider web' called Business Intelligence. One of the first objectives of the Business Intelligence audit will be to clearly identify and define all the parts and describe the whole of Business Intelligence.

3. Assess Risks and Rewards. An enterprise data warehouse and associated analytical services can absorb an enormous amount of money. Many in the industry have experienced first hand that this is the final burial place for millions of dollars and untold related lost jobs. It is important to identify the risks for the or-ganization involved in both the creation and use of the Business Intelligence. Opportunities may be lost without a good base of Business Informa-

tion. Identifying problems in the creation and management of the Business Intelligence assets is key to improvement. And, of course, it is equally important to know exactly how and what kind of positive results can accrue. Busi-ness Intelligence assets can actually ensure the success of a company or contribute to failure.

4.   Manage Business Intelligence Assets. How does organization management effectively apply resources? Where exactly should the dollars, time and human resources be spent to obtain the greatest value. In addition, there are opportunities to reduce the amount of replication between systems, thereby saving storage (primary and backup), maintenance fees, technician costs, and more.

5.   Improve Business Intelligence. Business Intelligence assets are quite possibly the most crucial assets which the organization can own. There is little doubt of the value inherent in giving the people in the company better information, in easy to use for-mats, and in a timely manner, i.e. at the time they need it to do their jobs. An audit will pinpoint specific areas of weakness and strengths in the Business Intelligence structure and functions. These identified points of inter-est can then be effectively addressed in a program for improvement.

4. The Business Intelligence Capability Maturity Model

The Business Intelligence Capability Maturity Model has been cre-ated in order to define and guide an audit, assessment and rating of Business Intelligence Assets. This Business Intelligence Capability Maturity Model is a set of blueprints, maps, graphics and constructs which may be used by an organization as a comprehensive guide to the audit of Business Intelligence assets.

Capability Maturity Model History.
The first Capability Maturity Model (CMM) in Information Systems was created for the purpose of developing and refining software development processes. A major purpose of this Software Development model was to allow for assessing the capabilities of organizations who wished to do business with the military and government. Assessing a company against the model allowed for the rating of the organization in terms of the level of maturity in software development. This assessment was used to determine the capabilities of the organization against industry standards. However, providing for Business Intelligence for an organization is not the result of a set of processes found in the typical software development. Therefore, the Capability Maturity Model for Business Intelligence must be different in many respects. It should be noted, though, that the rationale, and use of such a model is very similar.

5. Using the Business Intelligence Audit Results

The results of The Business Intelligence Audit can be of crucial importance to the organization. Some of the benefits of a Business Intelligence Audit were defined in Section 3 of this chapter. In this section, we look at using the Audit results. Some of the key areas are identified which may be directly impacted by using the results of the audit are noted in this section.

Improvement of Business Intelligence creation and management.
A primary interest will be in using the specific results to plan and implement a program for improvement.

Organization Level of Maturity. Another result will be to give management some idea of their relative 'score' in relation to the rest of the industry in terms of creation and management of Business Intelligence Assets. Whatever the Level of Maturity ranking, this should not be of paramount interest to management. This **may be** a difficult principal to apply. However, it is important to remember the goals which should be defined at the beginning of the audit process. These should be specific reasons which prompted the audit and what results are expected and how those results should be viewed and used. The more important aspects of the Business Intelligence Audit are related to understanding and improving the Business Intelligence Asset Base.

Should management concentrate on 'improving' the Level of Maturity ranking for the organization? That depends on the reason and methods to be used to make such industry competitive ranking improvements. Certainly, creating and working through an Action Response Program (as defined in the Business Intelligence Capability Maturity Model) will improve the overall organization industry rank. However, 'bragging rights' should not be the goal.

Understanding of the Business Intelligence Asset Base. Perhaps the most important and most useful of the results from the audit is the new understanding which is gained regarding the Business Intelligence Asset Base. Now management will be able to see through the morass and complexities of business intelligence structures, infrastructures, constructs, and general noise. It will be clear exactly what is included in the Business Intelligence Asset Base and what are the relationships of the parts.

Manage Business Intelligence Assets. Development of strategic and tactical plans for creation and management of Business Intelligence is difficult at best. A Business Intelligence Audit can give a more definitive understanding and definition to the key aspects for getting the most value from the Business Intelligence assets. The results can point to more practical and value-added planning for resource utilization. The audit results should also point out some clear directives in terms of areas such as - software and hardware direction and use; service level agreements; user interfaces and satisfaction; support and maintenance; security and governance and the Business Intelligence Development process.

Security. Business Intelligence is arguably the most important asset which an organization owns. Determining how well these assets are secured should be an integral part of the Business Intelligence Audit.

CHAPTER **2**

BUSINESS INTELLIGENCE

Chapter Contents
1. Defining Business Intelligence
2. Business Drivers
3. Classifying Business Intelligence
4. The Business Intelligence Performance Feedback Cycle
5. More about Business Intelligence Technologies

1. Defining Business Intelligence

Business Intelligence is an industry term which generally refers to the business information within an organization which is used to monitor, report on, analyses and for understanding and improving the business, i.e. for decision making. Business Intelligence applications are those which allow for identification, location of the relevant data, both internal and external, and the translation of that data into business information which can be leveraged by the people and interfacing systems into knowledge for better management. The base for Business Intelligence within an organization comes from information technology assets as well as business resources. Business Intelligence has several constructs and components. It is a complex set of architectures, a collection of integrated applications and data bases, plus all the associated standards, policies, procedures, protocols, communications. Business Intelligence also includes, in large part, the interfacing business acumen of the human resources, i.e.

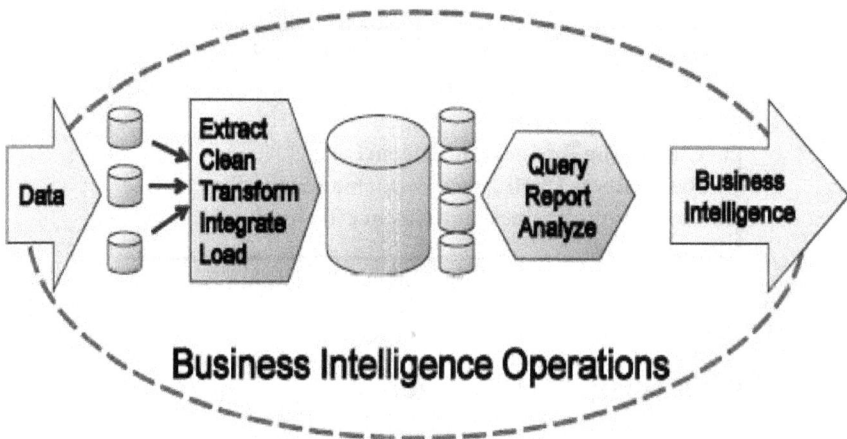

Business Intelligence Operations

1. Defining Business Intelligence

Business Intelligence is an industry term which generally refers to the business information within an organization which is used to monitor, report on, analyses and for understanding and improving the business, i.e. for decision making. Business Intelligence ap¬plications are those which allow for identification, location of the relevant data, both internal and external, and the translation of that data into business information which can be leveraged by the people and interfacing systems into knowledge for better management. The base for Business Intelligence within an organization comes from information technology assets as well as business resources. Business Intelligence has several constructs and components. It is a complex set of architectures, a collection of integrated applications and data bases, plus all the associated standards, policies, procedures, protocols, communications. Business Intelligence also includes, in large part, the interfacing business acumen of the human resources, i.e. the people, who interact with and help to translate the resulting information into useful and sometimes phenomenal business advantage. In this book, we refer to this complex set of Business Intelligence components as the Business Intelligence Asset Base.

Within this book, we identify as Business Intelligence almost any information technology system and associated data which is NOT defined as a transaction based or operational system. Operational systems are used in those daily activities and transactions which are related to the manufacture, sale and accounting for the products of an organization. These transaction systems provide for the structure and basic operations for the organization. The utilization of the resulting data, along with external and other relevant data, in the review, monitoring, analysis and planning for the organization is referred to in this book as Business Intelligence.

History and rationale for Business Intelligence.

Increasingly, operational systems and evolving technologies have led to vast amounts of data becoming available. Collection and use of that data became a major challenge. Organizations have been overwhelmed. The operations data systems which collected the data were numerous and varied. Data formats and storage of the trans-action data are mostly incompatible. Any analysis of the data col-lected was difficult and extremely time consuming. Reports could take a long time.

Data Warehouses have been developed and evolved to the point where the data can be collected, cleaned, translated, integrated. Turn¬ing the raw data into quality business information is much more eas¬ily accomplished. Improved technologies to extract the source data and move it quickly and integrate it have increased the speed and performance of the process. Online Analytical Processing (OLAP) and other reporting technologies have allowed faster generation of new reports which analyze the data. Business intelligence has now become the art of sifting through large amounts of data, extracting pertinent information, and turning that information into knowledge upon which action can be taken.

Scope and Breadth of Business Intelligence.
An organization can benefit from Business Intelligence in truly astounding ways. We generally think of the query and reporting, i.e. the analytics involved with the desk top Business Intelligence toolsets, like Cognos, as the Business Intelligence applications for the organization. However, Business Intelligence is really played in a much broader arena. In most cases, the primary source for business intelligence is a common repository of integrated, cleansed business information, e.g. an Enterprise Data Warehouse. A variety of Business Intelligence query, reporting and analysis tools are usu¬ally available. Depending on the sophistication and the needs of the user, the Business Intelligence is available in multiple forms.

2. Business Drivers

Organization management invests in Business Intelligence for a number of reasons. A primary reason may be the successful results shown by other organizations. There are also a number of differ¬ent business drivers which demand excellent Business Intelligence. These are strong motivators for providing the best possible systems and information.

Business Planning & Management
Looking at the business as a whole, the improvements which can be made in planning and directing the organization can be a major incentive.

Competitive Advantage
Increasingly, organizations must survive in a global economy. Com-

petition is stiff and can easily drown the enterprise. The company needs to have whatever it takes to overcome that competition. The best in Business Intelligence can be the deciding factor.

Cost Management

Business Intelligence systems can greatly expand on the capabilities of standard costs and finance systems. Business Intelligence sys¬tems can now, for example, identify spending patterns and provide the means for analysis and improvements. From expense reporting to vendor negotiations - there are tangible cost savings available with today's business intelligence capabilities.

Customer Management

Customer relationship management is a primary application for Business Intelligence today. These Business Intelligence systems have made a tremendous difference in management of customers, from the actual interface to the use of buying habit analysis in marketing.

Performance Management

Improving and managing operations are key drivers for the Business Intelligence investment for an organization. Management and improvement of operations has always been a key motivator in the development of Business Intelligence Systems. Most of the reporting and analysis relates to particular aspects of operations within the organization, In most cases, there has been a human interface, i.e. using the Business Intelligence for 'feedback' into the operational areas. However, in an increasing number of instances, the interface is automated and feedback and operational change may be the result of these automated systems. This performance management arena is more difficult to identify, audit and provide a tangible assessment than is possible within finance and customer relations. Still, this is a significant business driver (i.e. motivator) for Business Intelligence. There are a number of other areas where Business Intelligence is particularly critical. The application areas are expanding as the field grows. Arenas like the manufacturing floor are most likely next on the lists for heavy duty exploration and business improvement.

3. Classifying Business Intelligence

Information Technology Systems

The information and associated information technology systems within an organization can be classified based on function. There are three primary functions - Operational; Business Intelligence;

and Business Performance Management. These are defined and described as follows:

1. Operational - Structured systems which are used in all the activities and transactions involved in creating, selling, and accounting for the products of the organization.

2. Business Intelligence - Operational, legacy and external data which has been cleansed, integrated and translated into quality information which can be used by the organization to manage and improve activities and operations.

3. Business Performance Management - Technology is moving toward the capability for accessing the business information and then automating the use and feedback of results back into the operations, i.e. taking out the human interven¬tion and automatically leveraging the business information for improvement. The current reality is that action and use of the Business Intelligence in nudging and improving the business is mainly through the manual intervention of the human resources involved. However, there are some very real expectations and some experience which indicate that by applying predesigned and architected Business Rule models and through emerging technologies, the industry will be able to automate feedback and jump this gap into true automation.

Business Intelligence Systems

There are a number of different categories of Business Intelligence interface and utilization -- Scorecards and Dashboards; Reporting; Online Analytical Processing (OLAP); Advanced analysis and forecasting; and notifications to users based on preset event or threshold triggers. All these Business Intelligence categories will be discussed in the chapter on Analytics.

Business intelligence software incorporates the ability to mine data, analyze information, and report and feedback changes into organization structures and operations. Some modern Business Intelligence software allow users to cross-analyze and perform research for better analysis of sales or performance on an individual, department, or company level. Managers can now rapidly develop reports for forecasting, analysis, and business decision making. Business intelligence often uses Key Performance Indicators (KPIs) to as¬sess the present state of business and to feedback and fine tune the operations. This Business Intelligence methodology has been en-hanced and extended by Business Intelligence to the point where not only do we report what is happening, but can frequently identify the causes.

Business Intelligence End User Tools
Business Intelligence end user tools fall into several categories -

- Reporting - advising the appropriate users - what has happened in the business. These may be reports on operations, including exception reports and scorecards, for example. Usually standard, pre designed reports are developed and made available for those requirements which are relatively stable and of a continuing nature. The users of these reports may have no other need to interface with the organization Business Intelligence systems. Easy of use and simplicity are probably most important for these users.

- Monitoring - tracking and reporting on what just happened. This may be, for example, in the form of pre designed templates as 'dashboards' and triggers and alerts. (i.e. Other · spectrum from standard, pre designed reports, are those users and tools which allow for complex mining and analysis ofthe Business Intelligence resources for everything - forecasting to understanding, demographics and statistics on customers and competitors.

- Prediction - What will happen? Currently only a tiny portion of the Business Intelligence applications cover this area -- e.g. forecasting and simulation.

set Goals

BI feedback

Improve

- strategic,
- tactical, and
- operational.

Use Categories of Business Intelligence

We can also categorize Business Intelligence based on how and where it is used in the organization. Some of these categories based on use are:

Strategic Business Intelligence can be used in business planning and tracking for aligning the business to the long term goals and objectives of the organization. Long term could indicate weeks, months or even years. Senior management uses this strategic Busi-ness Intelligence to track the performance of the organization. One form of this Business Intelligence is as Key Performance Indicators, triggers and feedback on the organization results in the form of re-ports. Long term planning could include such goals as improving market share and product/unit profitability.

Tactical Business Intelligence is used by managers and analysts to measure and assist in improvement of short term operational performance. The feedback may be in the form of, for example, performance monitoring and measurements like dashboards and score-cards - over days or weeks.

Operational Business Intelligence. A current thrust in the technology initiatives for Business Intelligence is the capability of monitoring and impacting performance of daily operations. This very short term feedback is based on 'right time' Business Intelligence. This data is most often extracted from daily operations in real time or near real time, with a rapid translation and integration through vir-tual or federated views or into a repository such as an Operational Data Store - fast path information of use to those who need it to impact current operations. We will discuss later how some of the technologies and methodologies, including push and pull data meth-ods of extraction, are moving rapidly toward satisfaction of some of these business requirements.

4. The Business Intelligence Performance-Feed-back Cycle.

When used most effectively - there is a Business Intelligence reporting and feedback cycle which leverages Business Intelligence in the improvement of management and operations of the business. In some few cases, this feedback and improvement may be auto¬mated. However, with the state of the current technology, in most cases the human resources who see and use the Business Intelligence make the changes which impact the subsequent operations. This performance-cycle can deliver some very impressive benefits for an organization. The change and improvement roles are mainly intuitive and result automatically from the reporting to the appropriate staff and management. However, an organization management and staff which recognizes the inherent capabilities for feedback and improvement in operations and alignment against both short term and long term goals is the organization which can best leverage their business information for competitive advantage.

5. More about Business Intelligence technologies

It may be useful to take a look at Business Intelligence from the perspective of the myriad applications and technologies which are included under the Business Intelligence umbrella. The underlying Business Intelligence technologies are used to gather and analyze large quantities of unstructured data, and in transforming that data into information which can be used in understanding the operations and the business of an organization. In most cases, an organization has a data warehouse, or centralized staging area, for collection of all data to be used in the Business Intelligence arena. The data is extracted from the numerous data sources on a periodic basis. However, the industry appears to be moving on to a level of process based, real time (i.e. right time) decision support of many activities across the organization. In these cases, the data is most often 'pushed' into a special segment of the data warehouse, called the Operational Data Store. These technologies are in early stages and involve event driven triggers or change data transfer methods which capture changes to the operational data.

Different organizations have different requirements from Business Intelligence applications, and there are a wide range of available technologies and tools to meet these needs. These range from Query and Reporting by and for business end users to extensive analysis and forecasting. Some Business Intelligence applications are used to analyze performance of operations and extended business activities. Some examples are - Score carding, activity monitoring, strategic and tactical planning, competitor analysis. Business Intelli¬gence may be funneled into comprehensive Executive Information Systems. The vendor offerings include Finance and Budgeting tools and extensive others, such as those used to store and analyze data, for Data Mining and Forecasting. We may also consider within the scope of the Business Intelligence Asset Base the unstructured data within Content Management Systems, Document warehouses and Document Management Systems. However for the purposes of this book, we will not focus on these 'unstructured data' technologies.

To further highlight the extensive range of Business Intelligence offerings and solutions for an organization -following are a few more examples of the Business Intelligence technologies in use today: Geographic Information Systems, Dashboarding; Management Information Systems, Trend Analysis, Online Analytical Processing (OLAP) and analytics based on the aggregated 'cube' formats of some of the Business Intelligence tools. Statistics and Technical Data Analysis including not only unstructured data analysis and mining, but also Web Mining and Text mining If we look more closely at applications such as Customer Relationship Management (CRM) and Marketing tools and Human Resources applications, we see Business Intelligence in action. All these and more can be considered as Business Intelligence applications.

3

The Business Intelligence Capability Maturity Model

1. Introduction

The TBIA Business Intelligence Capability Maturity Model™ has been developed to allow an organization to evaluate how well it is doing in the creation and management of Business Intelligence assets. A well designed Capability Maturity Model can be used as a blueprint and can provide benchmarks for assessing the performance of an organization in creation, delivery and use of Business Intelligence.

The TBIA Business Intelligence Capability Maturity Model™ is a map and a guide to the assessment of Business Intelligence assets. The model establishes a common language and creates ground rules. It sets the standards, defines the path and describes how to accomplish an audit and how to use the results. Industry experience and best practices are used as the standard for instruction and assessment.

Standardized Tools and Methods. Using the TBIA Business Intelligence Capability Maturity Model™ allows the organization management to assess Business Intelligence assets using standardized tools and methods. Without some industry guidelines and standards, a Business Intelligence audit would be of questionable value to the organization. With the pressing need for more and more Business Intelligence, the limited resources, until now, have been primarily allotted to creating and maintaining those Business Intelligence assets. However, this set of Audit tools, methods, and standards should allow an organization to place a high priority on conducting a Business Intelligence Audit. Determining how well Business Intelligence is being created and used and comparing this assessment against the industry norms will be extremely valuable to the organization and can provide a firm base for planning and action.

Evaluation Capabilities. Clearly defined audit evaluation results can pinpoint strengths, weaknesses and help to define and clarify areas which need improvement. The TBIA Business Intelligence Capability Maturity Mode™ is intended as a foundation for an organization to accomplish at least the following:

· Understand the nature and the full extent of the Business Intelligence assets within the organization.
· Measure the relative accomplishment of an organization in re-

lation to the industry, i.e. in terms of integration and use of currently available Business Intelligence technology, business components and knowledge basics.

· Clarify the effectiveness of the Business Intelligence resources within the organization; i.e. how well are those resources being used to provide for the information requirements of the business decision makers.

· Create and outline a methodology to quantify capabilities of the organization in measurable and descriptive terms which can provide a base for proactive improvement, i.e. identify and assess strengths and weaknesses. This will set a starting point for continuing to monitor, assess and improve Business Intelligence assets.

· Identify risks inherent in current Business Intelligence goals and practices.

· Describe and provide measurement objectives for each component of the Business Intelligence Asset Base of an organization.

2. What is the Business Intelligence Capability Maturity Model ?

The TBIA Business Intelligence Capability Maturity Model™ is a framework and blueprint of Business Intelligence for the organiza tion. The model is a structured collection of all the components which make up the Business Intelligence assets for an organization. The model includes a taxonomy and clear descriptions. It describes the relationships among all those components. The TBIA Business Intelligence Capability Maturity Model™ also provides some industry standard characteristics and guidelines against which the organization assets may be measured.

The TBIA Business Intelligence Capability Maturity Model™ has been created in order to define and guide an audit, assessment and rating of Business Intelligence assets. This TBIA Business Intelligence Capability Maturity Model™ is a set of blueprints, maps, graphics and constructs which may be used by an organization as a comprehensive guide to the audit of Business Intelligence assets.

3-A

TBIA Business Intelligence Capability Maturity Model'

Objectives

1.   Identify and Define **What to Measure**
2.   Create **Measurement Factors**
3.   Define a **Measurement Scale**
4.   Define an **Audit Metholodgy**
5,   Describe How to **Use the Audit Results**

TBIA BUSINESS INTELLIGENCE CAPABILITY MATURITY MODEL™

Section 1: What to Audit

Understanding the exact nature and composition of the Business Intelligence Asset Base is the key first step in any audit. The Business Intelligence Asset Base includes all the constructs, components and systems which need to be considered when auditing the organization Business Intelligence capabilities.

The Business Intelligence Asset Base

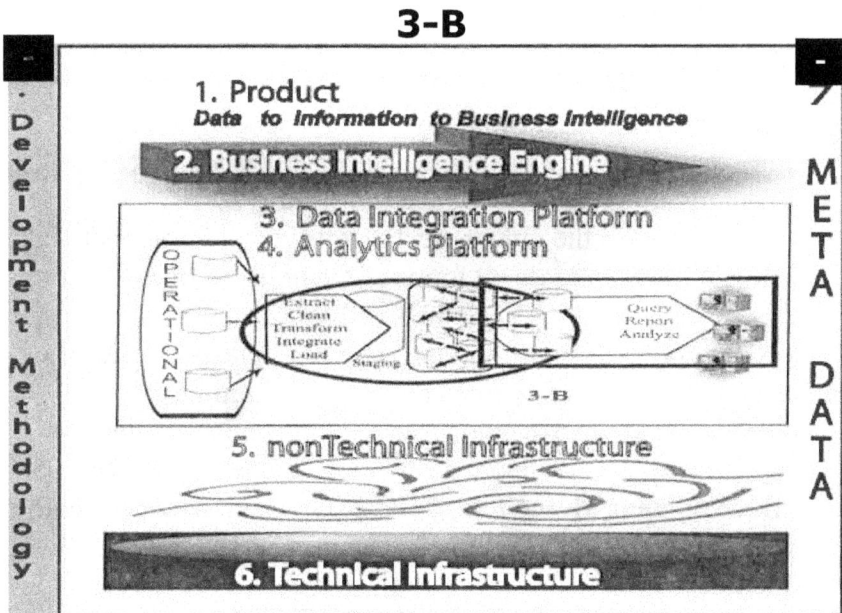

3-B

The Business Intelligence Asset Base should be viewed and understood as the complete and unified set of constructs and components which comprise Business Intelligence (see 3-C).

The primary components of the Business Intelligence Asset Base are:

· **Data Integration Platform** - A place where data is collected and integrated into a usable library of information. In most cases, this is the Enterprise Data Warehouse.

· **Analytics Platform** - This includes all user interfaces to the information library and all the analysis, query and reporting for use of the information.

· **Business Intelligence Engine** - The Business Intelligence Engine is responsible for the collection of data, translation into information and Business Intelligence and movement across the organization.

· **Technical Infrastructure** - The base foundation of hardware, software, middleware, communications, data base management systems and meta data management systems.

· **nonTechnical Infrastructure** - The second layer of the infrastructure, which includes such constructs as standards, guidelines, training, governance and security.

· **Data** - Data is the raw product. However, in this model, the term data encompasses all forms of the product, from the raw data to the final form, Business Intelligence.

· **Meta Data** - The information about the data. Although meta data has been presented as a separate component. The information product is composed of both the data component and the meta data component.

• **Development Methodology** - The processes, methods and standards and guidelines used in the creation of Business Intelligence.

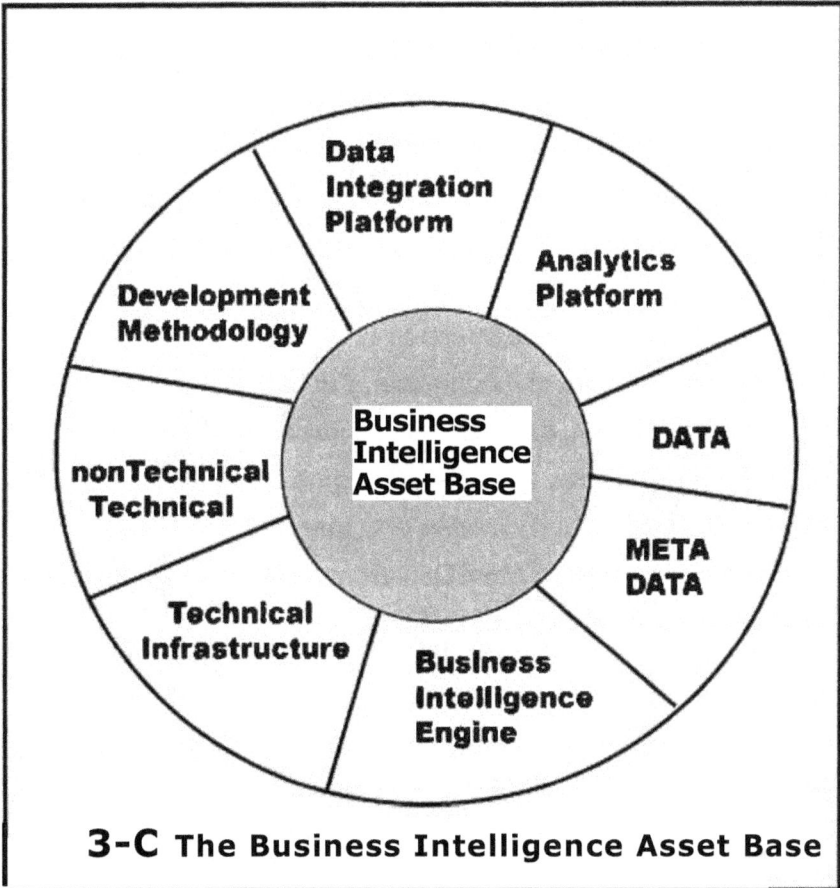

3-C The Business Intelligence Asset Base

Key Assessment Features

Each component of the Business Intelligence Asset Base can be further decomposed into its relevant parts and features. These are the Key Assessment Features. They are most often specific to the component and can be used to more fully understand and audit that component of the Business Intelligence Asset Base.

In a few cases, some of the Key Assessment Features may be replicated and that Key Assessment Feature is shown as integral to several different Business Intelligence Asset Base components. These duplications have been made in order to review those features from different perspectives. The intention is to make the review and assessment more relevant and complete. For example, meta data is a stand alone component, but it is also considered as a Key Assessment Feature for the Business Intelligence Engine and, in addition, is included in the Data, as well as, other components. These replications should allow the review of Meta Data from different perspectives and in conjunction with closely related topics.

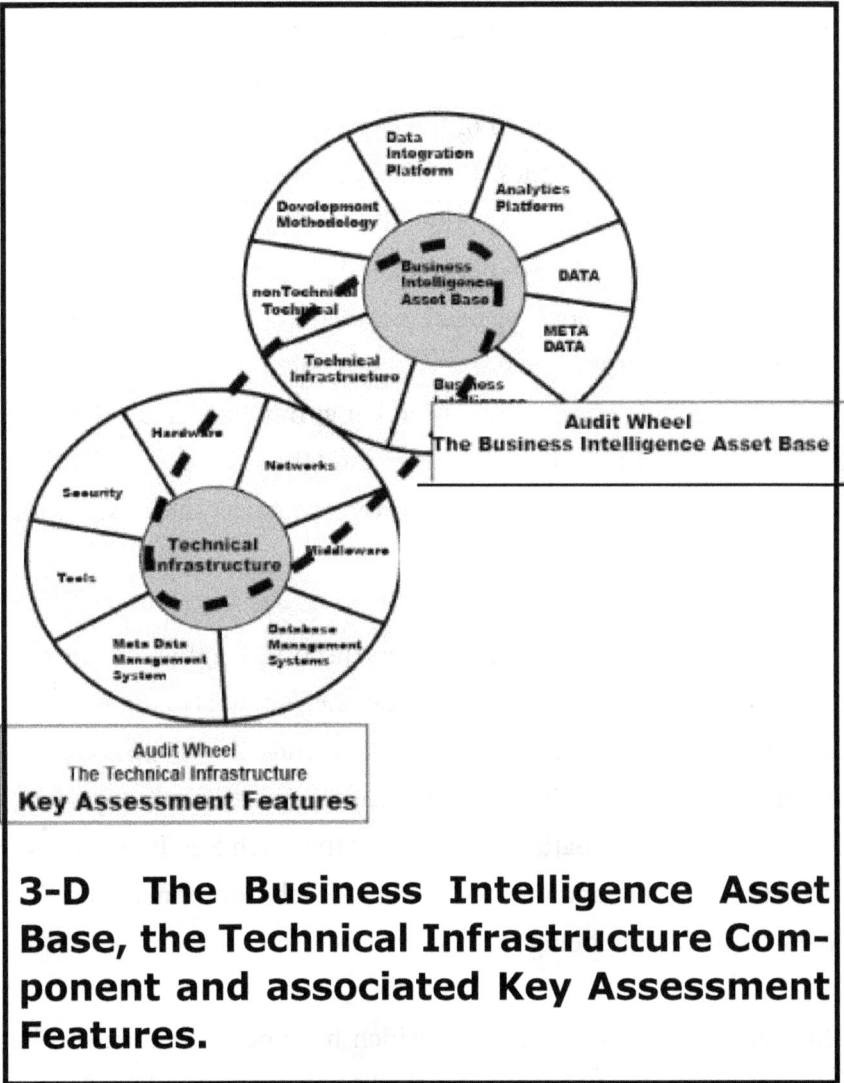

3-D The Business Intelligence Asset Base, the Technical Infrastructure Component and associated Key Assessment Features.

Section 2: Key Performance Indicators

The Key Performance Indicators are audit factors which are used to rate each of the Key Assessment Features, each of the Business Intelligence Asset Base components, as well as, the overall Business Intelligence Asset Base. Each of the Key Performance Indicators are used to measure the Business Intelligence assets just as height would be used to measure a person. The KPI's include both Business and Technology aspects. The definitions and descriptions of these Key Performance Indicators have been included in Chapter 8. These Key Performance Indicators may have to be redefined or refined based on the organization requirements and environment. This will mean that the audit team should fully understand the concepts so that they can modify the Key Performance Indicators to meet the needs of the organization.

The Business Intelligence Audit process discussed in this chapter and the remainder of the book includes a detailed analysis of the Key Performance Indicators as they are relevant to and impact each Key Assessment Feature and Business Intelligence Asset Base component. This includes an evaluation of the extent that each Key Performance Indicator is present and incorporated into each Component and Key Assessment Feature being audited.

The Key Performance Indicators which have been identified to be used for the Business Intelligence Audit are shown in Chart 3-E on the following page. Each of these Key Performance Indicators are defined and described in detail in later chapters.

3-E   Key Performance Indicators

Management Support
Business - IT partnership
Business Alignment
Satisfaction of Goals
Integration
Scalability
Adaptability
Performance
Simplicity, Flexibility,
Ease of Use
Comprehension
Quality
Value

Section 3: Ruler for Measurement

In order to complete The Business Intelligence Audit, there must be some scale to use as a standard for measurement of organization assessment results. Extending the previous example, with height as the measurement factor, this Levels of Maturity scale is used like a corresponding ruler. This ruler, however, measures how well the organization is creating and managing Business Intelligence. This scale for measurement of Business Intelligence assets has been created using industry best practices and current standards as

> # Levels of Maturity
>
> Level 1 - Initial
> Level 2 - Elementary Integration
> Level 3 - Enterprise Effective
> Level 4 - Optimized
> Level 5 - Leader
>
> ## 3-F

a base. These industry standards and best practices are defined, described and grouped into categories which can be used to rank the capabilities of an organization. Each level of the scale is defined and described in relationship to the Business Intelligence components, Key Assessment Features, and the overall organization. This means that each category is defined as a set of tangible expectations and guidelines for each of the Key Assessment Features, components and overall Business Intelligence asset base. These are selected and fit into categories to reflect recognized industry practices. The categories have been defined to incorporate specific levels of accomplishment. (See Chapter 6, Levels of Maturity)

Each category includes a range of constructs and practices which are clearly defined and described. The constructs and practices in each category are carefully selected for uniformity and to fit within a defined range of effectiveness and quality.

The effectiveness of the organization is defined by matching the results from the Business Intelligence audit for the organization with the ruler, i.e. the measurement categories in the Levels of Maturity Scale.

There are two sets of measurement scales for The Business Intelligence Audit Process.

1. **Levels of Maturity** -- How well an organization creates and manages Business Intelligence is determined by a comparison of the results of The Business Intelligence Audit against the scale for ranking the organization against the industry guidelines, standards and best practices. This is the measurement scale which allows for ranking of the organization.

2. **Rating Scale for the 'Target of Audit'** - This is the scale which is used to measure the Key Assessment Features and Components of the Business Intelligence Asset Base. This scale is used during the audit process and during the evaluation of the first and second level audit targets. This scale is similar to the Levels of Maturity for the whole of the organization. However, the scale starts at 0, zero, which indicates that the Key Assessment Feature or Component is not present; Zero may also indicate that the Key Performance Indicator under review is not present within the Key Assessment Feature or Component.

Each of the Key Assessment Features and the Components of the Business Intelligence Asset Base are scored individually using the Target Rating Scale. Then the organization is scored using the Levels of Maturity and a Level of Maturity Rank is assigned to the organization.

Levels of Maturity

Following are the Levels of Maturity which have been defined in the TBIA Business Intelligence Capability Maturity Model™ for the creation and management of Business Intelligence assets for an organization. Included here is a brief description of the guidelines for rating an organization at each level. There are more detailed descriptions of each level shown in Chapter 6, Levels of Maturity. Each category is based on industry best practices and guidelines and refers to the Business Intelligence Asset Base, and the Components and Key Assessment Features.

Level 1. Initial. This is the lowest level of Business Intelligence capability for an organization. Only the basic structures for data collection into silos of data are present, usually at the department level. There is no trace of a data integration platform.

Level 2. Elementary Integration. Maturity Level 2 is primarily characterized by the presence of an initial or rudimentary Enterprise Data Warehouse along with departmental or localized data marts, or silos of data.

Level 3. Enterprise Effective. A primary characteristic of this level of Business Intelligence maturity is the presence of an effective Enterprise Data Warehouse. There are no data marts which are not integrated into the data warehouse, i.e. no silos of data.

Level 4. Optimized. An organization with a Business Intelligence level of maturity of 4 is creating and using Business Intelligence in a manner which provides excellent business decision support.

Level 5. Leader. Maturity Level 5 shows the aggressive action of expert management in the utilization of Business Intelligence for decision making within the organization. Not only has management ensured an Optimized environment, they have pushed forward to a leadership position. Now, there is a fully realized Enterprise Data Warehouse. There are also a number of the features and functions which indicate thinking and planning which match that of the leaders in the industry. For example, there may be:

- guided analytics,
- an integration into the Business Intelligence library of both structured and unstructured data,
- a new paradigm for 'right' time data, most likely along with interfaces to an Enterprise Service Oriented Architecture
- universal access, through portals
- a search engine, which matches the best of the web engines
- fully integrated meta data, with an enterprise level meta data repository

Section 4: The Audit Process

Auditing the Business Intelligence assets for an organization requires:
· clear descriptions of all the parts of the Business Intelligence Asset Base,
· standards for assessing and rating, and
· well defined procedures for planning and conducting the audit.

The materials focused on this section of the TBIA Business Intelligence Capability Maturity Model™ provide the recommended process for auditing of the Business Intelligence assets for an organization is outlined.

3-G

The Business intelligence Audit Process
1.   Identify Specific Goals for the Audit
2,   Develop an Audit Plan
3.   Define the Business Intelligence Assets
4.   Correlate organization constructs with those of the -MIA Business Intelligence Capability Maturity ModeFm
5.   Perform the Baseline Audit (initial Audit)
6.   Rate the Business Intelligence Asset Base, Including Components and Key Assessment Features
7.   Rank the organization
8.   Communicate Audit Results
9   Create an Action Response Program (ARP)
10.   Initiate, Conduct ,and manage the ARP
11.   Monitor Results
12.   Re-Audit

The Business Intelligence Audit Process is outlined in 3.G. The Audit Process will be discussed in greater detail in Chapter 4.

The basic units which are the initial targets of the Business Intelligence audit are the Key Assessment Features (shown in Figure 3-D) which, as noted in previous sections are the parts into which each of the Business Intelligence Asset Base Components are subdivided. One of the initial steps in the Business Intelligence Audit is to identify and select the Key Assessment Features within the organization. The model descriptions are compared and correlated to the organization to identify the matching constructs. Subsequent steps and actual results of the audit rely on the initial audit information and the analysis related to these Key Assessment Features. Then information is collected for each of these Key Assessment Features. These Key Assessment Features are the level one targets of the audit.

Audit Tools

The remainder of the book will describe all the audit targets, tools and processes required to accomplish a quality Business Intelligence Audit. In summary, there are a series of Audit Wheels™ which define the Key Assessment Features and Components of the Business Intelligence Asset Base. The results of the audit process are compiled into a series of Business Intelligence Audit Score-cardsTM, i.e. Ratings Charts. These Audit Scorecards™ include summary level ratings for each of the Key Assessment Features. The Key Assessment Features are rated using each of the relevant Key Performance Indicators. Then an overall rating for that component of the Business Intelligence Asset Base is made.

There is an Audit Scorecard™ for each of the components of the Business Intelligence Asset Base. On the Audit Scorecard shown in chart 3-H, i.e. for the Business Intelligence Asset Base, all the summarized scores from each of the component scorecards are entered. Then the overall ratings along with the audit documentation and the opinions and judgments of the auditors are analyzed. Using all the related audit results, the organization Level of Maturity ranking is determined. This ranking indicates what the audit results indicate about the maturity of the capabilities of the organization management in creating and managing Business Intelligence. The ranking is determined by how those results fit within the Business Intelligence audit 'ruler', i.e. the Levels of Maturity. The Level of Maturity for an organization denotes how well they are able to create and manage Business Intelligence.

3-H

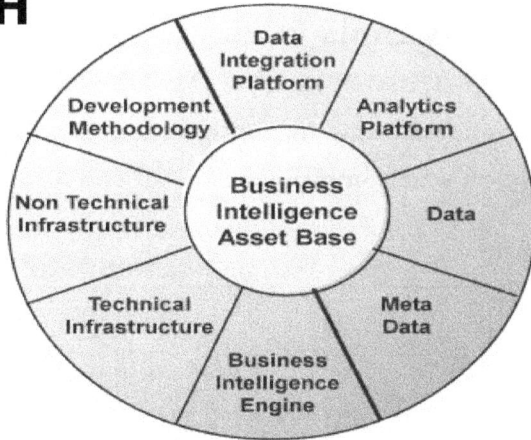

TBIA Audit Wheel™
The Business Intelligence Asset Base

3-I

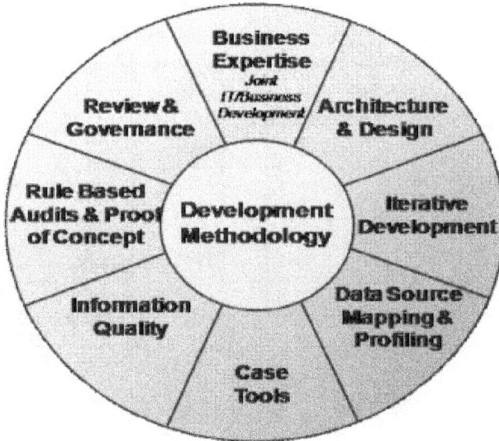

A component TBIA Audit Wheel™
The Development Methodology

The Audit Wheels™ are the graphic models which are used to guide and drive the audit process.

The TBIA Audit Scorecards™ are the collection tools which are used to gather and summarie the Audit Results. These charts allow for defined and easy organization and communications of the Audit Results.

Data Integration Platform

KEY PERFORMANCE INDICATORS

Rate each Key Assessment Feature of the Analytics Platform for each of the Key Performance Indicators. Use the Key Assessment Feature Ratings to derive the Overall Rating for the Asset Base. Ratings should be 1 - 5, with 5 as highest rating.

KEY ASSESSMENT FEATURES	Mangment	Support	BUSINESS ALIGNMENT	PARTNER SHIP	Business Goals	Scalability	INTEGRA TION	ADAPT ABILITY	PERFORM ANCE	USER FRIENDLY	COMPRE HENSION	QUALITY	VALUE
Platform Architecture													
Enterprise Architecture													
Data Architecture													
Data Models													
Meta Data													
Security													
Data Marts													
Data Integration Platform													

3-J

A TBIA Audit Scorecard™

for a Business Intelligence Asset Base Component
The Development Methodology

Rate each Component of the Business Intelligence Asset Base. This rating should reflect and summarize the detailed rating given for the Key Assessment Features for that Component. Use the Component Ratings to derive the Overall Rating for the Asset Base. Ratings should be 1 - 5, with 5 as highest rating	KEY PERFORMANCE INDICATORS														
	Management	Support Business	ALIGNMENT BUSINESS	PARTNER SHIP	BGoals Business	Scalability	INTEGRATION	ADAPTABILITY	PERFORMANCE	USER FRIENDLY	COMPREHENSION	QUALITY	VALUE
Data Integration Platform (Enterprise Data Warehouse)													
Analytics Platform													
Data													
Meta Data													
Technical Infrastructure													
NonTechnical Infrastructure													
Business Intelligence Engine													
Development Methodology													
Business Intelligence ASSET BASE													

ASSET BASE

3-K

A TBIA Audit Scorecard™
The Business Intelligence Asset Base

Section 5: Using the Audit Results

How should the organization use the results from an audit of Busi-ness Intelligence Assets? Some of the more practical uses of the Audit results are discussed in this section. These are just a few of the benefits which can be derived from a Business Intelligence Audit.

The Action Response Program (ARP).
The Audit Methodology in the TBIA Business Intelligence Capability Maturity Model™ includes a well defined program for using the results of the Business Intelligence audit. This Action Response Program is directed at improving the Business Intelligence Asset Base for the organization. Primary targets for this program are the specific audit results which indicate areas of excellence and those Key Assessment Features which need improvement. The Business Intelligence Audit should be conducted in such a manner that most of these specifics will be recognized during the phased approach to assessment. As these specifics are recognized during the audit, as much information, (or information sources, which can be later followed up during the ARP) should be collected as possible. (Note: Be sure this detailed collection for the follow-up specifics does not unduly slow down the audit process.)

Level of Maturity.
One result of the Business Intelligence Audit will be to give man-

agement some idea of their relative 'score' in relation to the rest of the industry in terms of creation and management of Business Intelligence Assets. Whatever the Level of Maturity ranking, this should not be the primary focus of interest for management. It is easy to say this, but very difficult to apply this in fact. Everyone likes to know how we compare with others in our industry, as well as, in the business world, in general. However, it is important to remember the goals which are defined at the beginning of the audit process. These should be specific reasons which prompted the audit, along with a clear expectation for the results and how those results should be viewed and used. The more important aspects of such an audit are related to understanding and improving the Business Intelligence Asset Base.

Should management concentrate on 'improving' the Level of Maturity ranking for the organization? That depends on the reason and methods to be used to make such industry ranking improvements. Certainly, creating and working through an Action Response Program will improve the overall organization industry rank. However, `bragging rights' should not be the goal.

Understand the organization Business Intelligence Assets
Perhaps the most important and most useful of the results from the audit is the new understanding which is gained regarding the Business Intelligence Asset Base. Now management will be able to see through the morass and complexities of business intelligence structures, infrastructures, constructs, and general noise. It will be clear exactly what is included in the Business Intelligence Asset Base and what are the relationships of the parts.

Manage Business Intelligence Assets.

Development of strategic and tactical plans for creation and management of Business Intelligence is difficult at best. A Business Intelligence Audit can give a more definitive understanding and definition to the key aspects for getting the most value from the Business Intelligence assets. The results can point to more practical and value-added planning for resource utilization. The audit results should also point out some clear directives in terms of such topics as - software and hardware direction and use; service level agreements; user interfaces and satisfaction; support and maintenance; security and governance and the Business Intelligence Development process.

Security

Business Intelligence is arguably the most important asset which an organization owns. Determining how well these assets are secured should be an integral part of the Business Intelligence Audit. The findings from the audit should be the base for an improvement program, if needed.

Quality Business Intelligence

A Business Intelligence Audit is a critical first step. but only a first step, in the effective management of Business Intelligence Assets. Once the initial documentation and assessment has been accomplished and the rankings have been determined, the foundation is established. Now management truly has a starting point for managing and delivering Business Intelligence which is of the highest quality, which meets the organization requirements and has an excellent rating in terms of cost to the organization versus value received.

CHAPTER 4

The Audit Process

Chapter Contents
1. Introduction
2. Audit Overview
3. Planning
4. Conduct the Audit
5. Rate the Organization
6. Use the Results

1. Introduction

The audit of Business Intelligence assets for an organization can be complex - as complex as the inherent nature of those assets. The goal is to make it as simple as possible. This book and the TBIA Business Intelligence Capability Maturity Model™ has been created to provide everything necessary to plan and conduct a Business Intelligence audit for the organization. Common business language is used throughout and all the terms should be clear, precise and understandable. The Business Intelligence Asset Base, along with all components and Key Assessment Features, i.e. parts, for the Business Intelligence components are identified and described. All the rating factors which should be used to review and assess each of the Business Intelligence components are identified and carefully defined. Guidelines and industry practices are discussed.

In this chapter, the method and processes which should be used for the audit are defined and described. There is also information on how to understand and use the tools provided by the Business Intelligence Capability Maturity Model™ in the audit of Business Intelligence assets of an organization.

2. Audit Overview

An Audit of the Business Intelligence assets for an organization should include the following:
A. Planning
    1.   Identify the scope and the goals of the audit.
    2.   Identify auditor(s) and team members.
    3.   Plan the Audit.
       · Identify the specific constructs, components, and features to be audited
       · Clarify, from the TBIA Business Intelligence Ca-pability Maturity ModelTM, the Key Assessment Features and other infor-

mation which pertain to the identified audit goals.

· Identify and review the appropriate Key Performance Indicators.

· Identify the organization constructs to be audited - based on correlation to the Business Intelligence Capability Maturity Model descriptions for each Key Assessment Feature and Component.

4. Review the audit and rating criteria.

B. Conduct the Audit

1. For each Component - and Key Assessment Feature - identify and define specific constructs within the organization which correlate with the TBIA Business Intelligence Capability Maturity Model™ definitions, i.e. define the specifics of the matching components and Key Assessment Features for the organization.

2. Gather documents and research Key Assessment Features and Business Intelligence Components.

3. Review research results.

4. Apply the Key Performance Indicators to the Business Intelligence Components and related Key Assessment Features and determine an initial rating for each applicable Key Performance Indicator to each component and feature.

5. Compare results to industry standards as defined in the Chapter 6 on Levels of Maturity and further described in each chapter which relates to the component or Key Assessment Feature.

C. Assess and Rate the organization

1. Assess and rate the organization Business Intelligence Asset Base components against the industry guidelines noted in the Business Intelligence Capability Maturity Model and Levels of Maturity rat-

ings and ranking guides.

2.   Assess and rate the organization Business Intelligence Asset Base overall, using the guidelines noted in the TBIA Business Intelligence Capability Maturity Model™ and Levels of Maturity ratings guide.

3.   Determine a Level of Maturity for the organization.

D.   Identify Organization Strengths

E.   Identify Organization Weaknesses

F.   Develop an Action Response Plan

Each of these steps needs careful review and clarification prior to beginning of the audit process.

3. Planning

Identify the scope and the goals of the audit.

Scope. The scope of an audit can include the complete Business Intelligence Asset Base or the scope of an audit may include only some part or parts of the asset base. The scope should be defined based on the requirements of the organization management, as well as, the time and resources available to apply to the audit. If there are specific concerns which are evident and the resources are limited, then the audit can be concentrated on assessing the areas of concern. This can be more effective and provide greater payback to the organization than attempting to taking on too much in any single project. These audits can be very complex and time consuming. It is much better to concentrate on what will provide the most return to the organization.

Goals. The expected returns on the audit investment dollar should be defined up front. These can be limited or very broad in nature and expectations of management and those involved should be set accordingly. An audit of Business Intelligence assets can be time consuming and expensive. However, the benefits can be substantial. For one thing, it is possible to identify problems which can be quickly resolved, once they are exposed and defined.

A few examples of audit goals are:
- To identify weaknesses and strengths within the Business Intelligence Asset Base.
- Provide a baseline for the continuing and improvement of Business Intelligence for the organization.
- Assess the quality and effectiveness of the Business Intelligence created and used within the organization.
- Assess risks for the organization inherent in the Business Intelligence processes.

The overriding business goals and the tangible, achievable goals of the audit are to understand the exact nature of Business Intelligence within the organization and to use that understanding to improve the creation, use of and quality of the Business Intelligence. Therefore, we may
- review specific parts of the Business Intelligence assets in order to better understand and enable improvement; or
- perform a full audit of the Business Intelligence Asset Base - to identify exactly what those assets are, how they fit together and how effective and valuable are the business intelligence products.

This full auidt will allow the organization to better understand the Business Intelligence assets, provide monitoring, and improve.

Politics

It is worth noting that any audit might take on political implications. These Business Intelligence audits are the kinds of projects which can impact jobs within the organization. The results should be treated as simply improvement opportunities. The audit manager and team need to at least be aware of the potential for political fall out.

Identify Audit Team

A full audit can be accomplished by one person, if the time allotted is long enough. If there is some urgency for completion - then up to three or more team members could be assigned. If it is more than a one person team, then there should be representation from both the information technology staff and the business staff. They do not necessarily have to be experts at any part of Business Intelligence, but these people do need to be analytical and able to investigate, analyze and communicate the information they obtain.

Plan the Audit

There should be a preliminary document which outlines goals, activities, and expected results from the audit. This document should be based on the goals as defined by the project 'sponsor', i.e. who ordered the audit. The business goals should be restated, then translated into specific audit goals. Some examples of what should be included:

· Take a look at the Business Intelligence Asset Base descriptions and identify any specific components to be reviewed. If the audit includes the whole of Business Intelligence - then list each of the components and each of the Key Assessment Features in the component.

· Read about and understand how the Key Performance Indicators fit into the assessment.

· Then, beside each of the components and Key Assessment Features in the list, identify and describe how the team intends to evaluate each one. Use the information in the remainder of this book as a starting point.

· Identify which of the Key Performance Indicators will be used for each component and Key Assessment Feature. Describe up front how that Key Performance Indicator influences or should be integrated into the feature or component.

· Use the model descriptions to provide a map of the actual process the audit team will use.

· Clarify and document the audit and rating criteria to be used

Review, re-review, then communicate the Business Intelligence audit plan.

4. Conduct the Audit

Identify the organization matching components.
For each component and for each Key Assessment Feature, identify the matching constructs within the organization. Review the model component to determine what to look for in the organization. Names of the departments and of the associated processes and contents should help. Talk to department management and staff to understand exactly what they do and ask them if they feel comfortable with the model designations.

Review and Analyze the organization constructs.
Decide how best to analyze each component and Key Assessment Feature. In many cases, the best way is to just ask users and those involved. Some other ways are to ask for and review documentation - e.g. computer logs and audit materials, which will document usage and performance. You may interview individuals or sponsor Focus Groups with particular subject areas as discussion topics. There may be experts, either on staff, or external, who can guide the auditors through specific areas or who can tell you what should be happening and what exactly is happening. For example, you may suspect that technical infrastructures are not scalable and you may find evidence of this in specific problems and 'break down's' which need to be understood. Identify and document the potential problems and track down the answers through interviews or 'expert' sources and documentation. For such an arena as capacity planning, you may document exactly how this is handled; then you may identify specific questions - e.g. Have the systems been able to keep up - or are there response time problems at

more than a few isolated peak times? Look for the Information Technology specialists who handle this? Ask them how and exactly what they do? Does it make sense? The questions should elicit reasonable answers which are easy to understand. If the answers are not easy to understand, then make the assumption that there is something further to explore. Even if the 'nitty gritty' is technical, there should be a good common sense explanation for what is included. The resulting answers should have clarity, be intuitive and make sense to an outsider. These are the kinds of explorations and analysis which will provide the answers required for quality audit results. Be sure to look for and review user contracts, i.e. service level agreements.

Apply the Key Performance Indicators.

Identify how each Key Performance Indicator impacts or is inte-grated into the organization component or Key Assessment Feature. Can you clarify and understand exactly how the KPI should be reflected in the organization for that construct? Ask the question -Does the Key Assessment Feature and/or component have the characteristics which are considered as crucial for that Key Performance Indicator?

5. Rate the Organization

Component Ratings.

Assess the organization construct against the model standards for the component and each of the Key Assessment Features. The component may be rated with an average of the features in total - or there may be some other considerations which make you rate the component slightly differently. You should use your own judgement here. In many cases, this becomes a subjective call. You, the auditor, have done the review. You need to be the one to decide the rating. Unlike financial audits, some of the assessment of Business Intelligence assets is not based on numbers from which 4 is easily derived from 2 and 2. Be sure to include in the audit planning list, a special notation to look for and include such items as Service Level Agreements and how well the particular group is performing against those agreements. Look also for user satisfaction and machine and software failures and inadequate responses.

Business Intelligence Asset Base Rating.

Use all the information gleaned from the audit process. Determine a rating based on an average of the ratings on all the asset components. Then take a look at the whole of the organization. How well are we doing, overall, in the creation, management and use of business intelligence and assets. What do you think? Determine the rating - then nudge or move the rating if necessary, based on your judgement. If you have done the audit properly, that judgement should include all the nuances and indications from the people you have interviewed and the detailed analysis and reviews. (Be sure to take extensive notes while performing the audit.) Some of the back up notes may not have been factored into the detailed reviews for the component. Trust your judgement. However, if you feel that the overall rating and the component average of sums is too different, you may need to reiterate , i.e. walk through the process again.

Using the Industry Guidelines.

During the whole of the analysis and rating process, it is important to continually compare findings with the industry guidelines and available documentation. During the review, the auditors should keep in mind and note how and what the organization what is doing and how it compares with the industry best practices.

Levels of Maturity

Level 1 - Initial
Level 2 - Elementary Integration
Level 3 - Enterprise Effective
Level 4 - Optimized
Level 5 - Leader

Determine a Level of Maturity for the Organization.

After all the gathering of information, assessment and analysis has been done, determining the Level of Maturity (i.e. 1 through 5) for the organization should be relatively straightforward. This should essentially equate to the overall rating from the previous step. (See Chapter 6, Levels of Maturity, for guidelines throughout the analysis and rating processes.) Both level 1 and level 5 are relatively easy to determine -- since there are definite restrictions on the criteria. Level 1 organizations do not have a data warehouse - but they do have existing local data marts, which have 'stand-alone' data. Level 5 organizations have a fully optimized data warehouse and analytical platform (i.e. meets and exceeds all expectations, industry standards and user requirements.) At level 5, however, an organization will also have many of the leadership features identified in Chapter 5.

6. Use the Results

Identify organization strengths and weaknesses.
Carefully review the audit process and results. Identify organization strengths and weaknesses. Do this at a detailed level. Make a list and describe the conditions and features which are exhibited by the organization. Describe why each point is considered a strength or weakness.

Place an estimated value on strengths and weaknesses.
Estimate the costs of the weaknesses in terms of risk to the organization. Where possible, estimate actual, tangible costs in terms of time, expense, human resources and unfulfilled Business Intelligence requirements. Define and elaborate on the 'pain points' and tangible examples of cost to the organization.

For the organization strengths - list them and describe each one, i.e. clarify exactly what steps or constructs the organization has which enhance their Business Intelligence management. Estimate the value to the organization of each identified strength in the Business Intelligence Asset Base.

Develop an Action Response Plan.
Analyze each of the strengths and weaknesses identified. What can be done to turn the weaknesses around? How can we capitalize on the strengths? How do we ensure that the identified strengths become a persistent and integrated part of the organization? Create a list of ac-

tions which can be taken. Prioritize these based on your evaluations of the risk and value factors involved.

Present the findings to management.

Use the TBIA Audit Scorecards and other graphics, or create a similar approach for a communications document for management and others. Be sure to create an executive level summary for any pre-sentation materials and for the paper with the Business Intelligence Audit results and details. The summary should include the highlights - i.e. organization Level of Maturity; Strengths and Weaknesses of the organization; Action Plan 'bullets'. Probably the most important part will be the graphics presentation of the results in a scorecard format.

Audit Tools and Guidelines

Chapter Contents

1. Using the Audit Tools and Guidelines

The templates and guidelines included in this chapter are intended to provide a foundation for the audit of the organization Business Intelligence assets. Special charts and tools have been created to be used in the assessment and rating process. These include

- Key Assessment Features - Level 1 audit targets. The Business Intelligence Asset Base is depicted, as a whole, then divided into components. Each Business Intelligence Component is then further subdivided into Key Assessment Features. These Key Assessment Features are the level 1 (lowest level) audit targets.

· **Audit Wheels**™ - The Audit Wheels™ are charts which identify all the components and Key Assessment Features of the The Business Intelligence Asset Base.

· **Key Performance Indicators** - these are the factors which have been identified in the Capability Maturity Model which are to be used in rating each Business Intelligence construct.

· **Audit Scorecards**™ - These are charts which are used to collect and summarize the ratings for the Business Intelligence audit.

All these Business Intelligence tools and graphics have been identified and defined in Chapter 3. The remainder of the book is devoted to providing more detailed descriptions and information about the Business Intelligence Audit. This chapter includes the templates, descriptions, guidelines on how to use them and where to find more information for assessing and auditing each construct.

2. Audit Guidelines

In planning for a comprehensive, quality audit of the Business Intelligence assets for an organization, the auditor should review all the materials and develop a plan based on that documentation. The high level plan has been defined in the previous chapter. The guidelines and suggestions in this section should be used in further detailing the audit plan.

Gather and review all documentation. Carefully review the chapters in this book and all the materials which have been gathered as a result of the planning process - as relevant materials which may be needed for the audit.

Create a list of topics to be included. Develop a list of all the items to be reviewed within the organization which correlate to that Business Intelligence Capability Maturity Model component. There is an Audit Wheel™ and a special chapter which covers each of the Business Intelligence components. Use these to compile the list for the audit. Incorporate any additional items into the list to make it comprehensive for your organization.

Identify organization constructs which correlate to the TBIA Business Intelligence Capability Maturity Model™ constructs. You should create a list which identifies all the constructs within the organization which relate to and are necessary to an analysis of each of the Key Assessment Features for each Business Intelligence Asset Base component. Continue the documentation with a short description of each of these features within the organization and exactly how it represents the constructs within your organization. For example, there may be 5 data marts which are under the umbrella of the Enterprise Data Warehouse and 2 which are stand alones. Under the appropriate Key Assessment Features within the Data Integration Platform component, identify and name each of these data marts in some way which will be recognizable by people in the your organization - i.e. by application or department. Describe them a little further with other information which will clarify what they are and who are the 'owners'.

Key Performance Indicators. Review Chapter 8 on topic of the Key Performance Indicators. Use these Key Performance Indicators to assess each Key Assessment Feature. For example, for each Data Mart ask the relevant questions about integration with the rest of the organization. In particular for a data mart - is this a department use (only) data mart, with the data as a stand alone or silo of data, i.e. not tied to a data warehouse library of information? Review and analyze the whole of the Business Intelligence Asset component in the same manner - i.e. apply each Key Performance Indicator to the whole component. In many ways, this is just a duplication of the efforts expended on the Key Assessment Features. However, this is the best way to ensure that everything necessary to the audit has been identified and included. The whole of the component, also, does not necessarily equal exactly the sum of the parts (Key Assessment Features.)

First Level Audit The Audit Wheel™ for the Business Intelligence Asset Base and the secondary Audit Wheel for the component, The Technical Infrastructure is shown in Figure 5-A. Note that the Key Assessment Features are depicted in the secondary Audit Wheel and there is a grey arrow indicating that the Key Performance Indicators are used for assessing each of these Key Assessment Features. Just as we may indicate a person's height as 5'8" and weight as 165 lbs -thus we would indicate that we rate the Scalabiliy Key Performance Indicator for the Hardware (Key Assessment Feature) at Level 3 for the organization.

5-A Level One Audit

Rate each Key Assessment Feature
Using each Key Performance Indicator

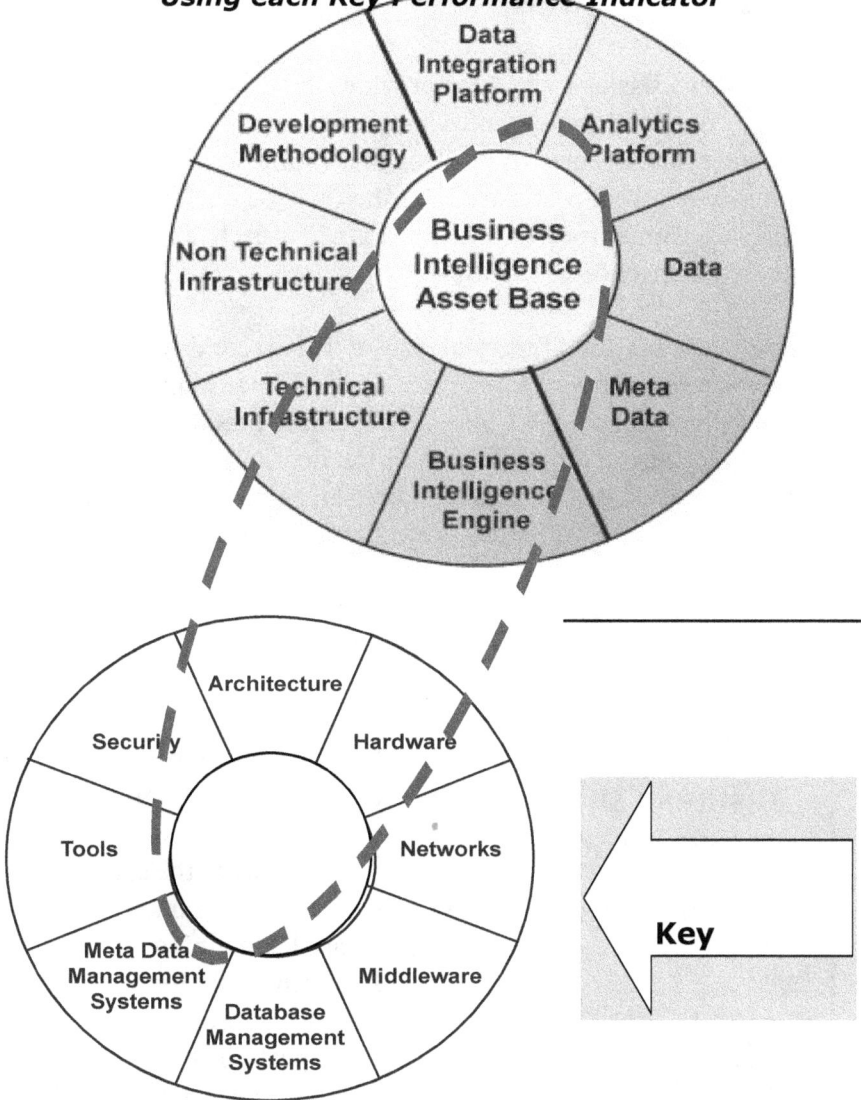

Data Integration Platform

Development Methodology

Analytics Platform

Non Technical Infrastructure

Business Intelligence Asset Base

Data

Technical Infrastructure

Meta Data

Business Intelligence Engine

Architecture

Security

Hardware

Tools

Networks

Meta Data Management Systems

Middleware

Database Management Systems

Key

3. Rating Scale

What is the Rating System?

There are two sets of scales. One provides the ruler for ranking of the capability of the overall organization in the creation and management of Business Intelligence assets. This first rating scale is described in Chapter 6, Levels of Maturity. The other is used during the Business Intelligence Audit process - as a scale for rating each of the parts of the Business Intelligence Asset Base.

Rating Scale for the 'Target of Audit' This second ratings scale is used to measure the Key Assessment Features and Components of the Business Intelligence Asset Base. This scale is used during the audit process and during the evaluation of the first and second level audit targets. This scale is similar to the Levels of Maturity for the whole of the organization. However, the scale starts at 0, zero, which indicates that the Key Assessment Feature or Component is not present; Zero may also indicate that the Key Performance Indicator under review is not present within the Key Assessment Feature or Component.

5-B
Business Intelligence Capability Maturity Model
Audit Rating Scale

Level 1 - Initial
Level 2 - Elementary Integration
Level 3 - Enterprise Effective
Level 4 - Optimized
Level 5 - Leader

The rating system functions like the school report card. There needs to be some uniform rating system which will apply to the audit results. The same rankings system used in defining the Levels of Maturity has been selected as most appropriate for rating all parts of the Business Intelligence Asset Base. Therefore, each component and Key Assessment Feature will be rated using these rating factors. The factors are discussed in more detail in Chapter 6 on the subject of Levels of Maturity. In that chapter, these ratings are applied to the overall Business Intelligence Asset Base for the organization. For each level, a detailed description of each possible rating, i.e. 1-5, has been written for each of the Components, Key Assessment Features, along with the corresponding Key Performance Indicators. These descriptions should prove valuable in determining a rating for the specific level 1 and level 2 (level 2 refers to the Component level rating.) audit targets. There are also audit guidelines for the detailed level audit in this chapter as well as in later chapters which are devoted to each of the components of the Business Intelligence Asset Base.

Rating Units
Following is a brief description of each rating level of the Audit Rating Scale for the audit targets. The ratings levels may apply to an individual Key Performance Indicator as applied to a Key Assessment Feature or Component. These ratings levels may also apply to the overall level of quality for a specific Key Assessment Feature or Component. More descriptions and details for the rating levels are discussed in Chapter 6.

Level 0: Not Present. The audit target* cannot be found

Level 1: Initial The audit target* being audited exists, but is very low in quality.

Level 2: Elementary Integration. There is some effective-ness, but relatively low quality found in the audit target*.

Level 3: Enterprise Effective. Equates to a 'fair to good' rating for the audit target* .

Level 4: Optimized. The audit target* is present and relatively well established and can be rated good to excellent.

Level 5: Leader. This is the top rating. The audit target* is present and can be considered to be ranked very high, i.e. with the industry leaders in this category.

—* **audit target is**, of course, whatever is being audited and rated. This will be any of the specific components, Key Assessment Features, or overall Business Intelligence Asset Base.

The basic units which are the initial targets of the Business Intelligence audit are the Key Assessment Features, which as noted in previous sections are the parts into which each of the Business Intelligence Asset Base components are subdivided. The Business Intelligence audit begins with the identification of these Key Assessment Features within the organization. This Step 1 of the Audit Methodology of the Business Intelligence Capability Maturity Model describes how to identify and select these Key Assessment Features for the organization. The model descriptions are compared and correlated to the organization to identify the matching constructs. Subsequent steps and actual results of the audit rely on the initial audit information and the analysis related to these Key Assessment Features. Step 2 of the Business Intelligence audit is the collection of information related to each of these Key Assessment Features. Each step of the audit is preplanned, based on information included in the TBIA Business Intelligence Capability Maturity Model™ along with realities of the organization, including constraints and opportunities.

5-C

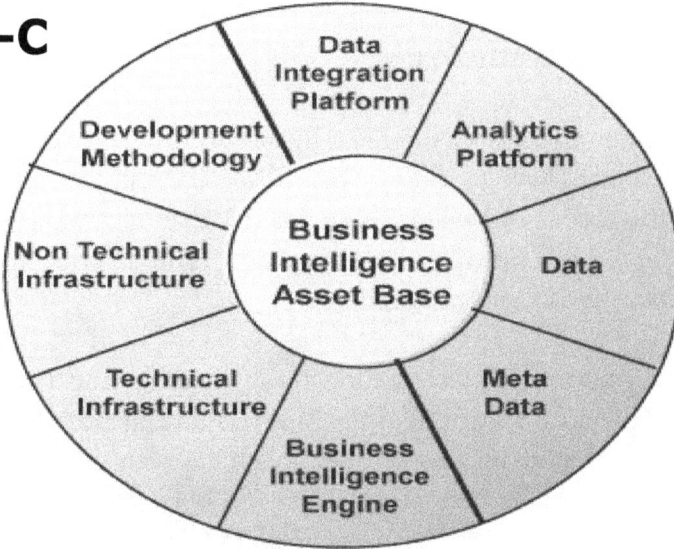

**A TBIA Audit Wheel™
The Business Intelligence Asset Base**

5-D

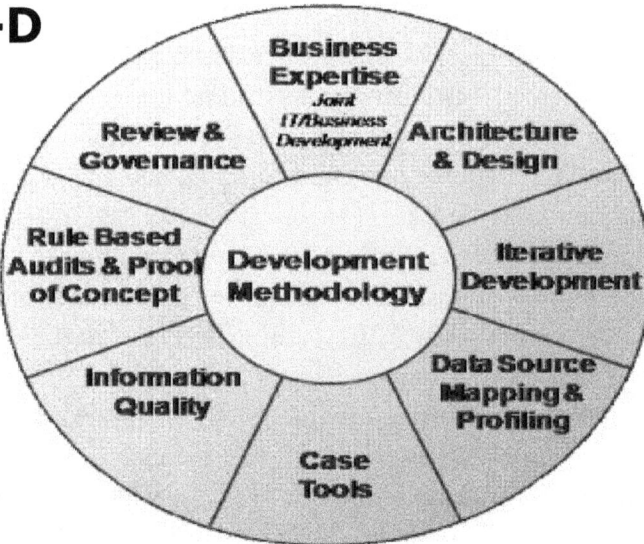

**A component TBIA Audit Wheel™
The Development Methodology**

4. Audit Tools: Audit Wheels™

The primary audit tools for the TBIA Business Intelligence Capability Maturity Model™ have been described in some detail in Chapter 3. Much of this discussion will duplicate that in Chapter 3. However, in this chapter, we will provide a little more detail and describe in more detail how these tools may be used.

The primary audit tools discussed in this chapter are the TBIA Audit Wheels™ which identify all of the Business Intelligence assets and should drive the audit process. The TBIA Audit Wheels™ are a series of charts which depict the Business Intelligence Asset Base, all its components and associated Key Assessment Features. These are described in Chapter 3, The Business Intelligence Capability Maturity Model.

Figure 5-B is an example of an Audit Wheel for the whole of the Business Intelligence Asset Base. This is the chart which depicts all the components of the Business Intelligence Asset Base and includes all the parts of Business Intelligence systems and assets throughout the organization. This includes the first level decomposition of the Business Intelligence Asset Base into eight components.

Each of these eight components are further divided into a second level of parts, called Key Assessment Features. See the example of the The Development Methodology TBIA Audit Wheel™ in Chart 5-C. These audit wheels are used to map the assets to be audited. These should direct the audit process by identifying exactly what needs to be identified in the organization and what should be analyzed. Each of the components is described in a number of places within this book, including Chapter 3 on the model constructs, as well as a special chapter devoted to each component. The documentation describes exactly what the component is, what it includes, some of the characteristics

5-E

Audit Scorecard™

The Business Intelligence Asset Base

KEY PERFORMANCE INDICATORS

Rate each Component of the Business Intelligence Asset Base. This rating should reflect and summarize the detailed rating given for the Key Assessment Features for that Component. Use the Component Ratings to derive the Overall Rating for the Asset Base. Ratings should be 1 - 5, with 5 as highest rating.	Mangment Support	BUSINESS ALIGNMNT	PARTNER SHIP	Business Goals	Scalability	INTEGRATION	ADAPTABILITY	PERFORMANCE	USER FRIENDLY	COMPREHENSION	QUALITY	VALUE
ASSET BASE												
Data Integration Platform (Enterprise Data Warehouse)												
Analytics Platform												
Data												
Meta Data												
Technical Infrastructure												
NonTechnical Infrastructure												
Business Intelligence Engine												
Development Methodology												
Business Intelligence ASSET BASE												

Audit Results include scorecards and Supporting Research & Documentation which are important to review during an audit and gives audit tips and notes. More detailed information is given in the chapters devoted to each component.

5. Audit Tools: Audit Scorecards™

The results of the audit process are compiled into a series of Business Intelligence Audit Scorecards™, i.e. Ratings Charts. These Audit Scorecards include summary level ratings for each of the Key Assessment Features. The Key Assessment Features are rated using each of the relevant Key Performance Indicators. Then an overall rating for that component of the Business Intelligence Asset Base is made. The Audit Scorecard™ is used to collect and document the audit results in a simple, convenient location. These Audit Scorecards™ provide a focus and some objectivity for the audit process and the compilation and presentation of the results. They also make it easier and faster to communicate the audit results in a straight forward, easy to understand manner.

Audit Scorecards™ for Business Intelligence Components. Just as there is an Audit Wheel™ for each of the Business Intelligence Asset Base Components, which maps and drives the audit process, there is an Audit Scorecard™ which is used to collect and summarize the results. The Audit Scorecard shown in 5-B is for the Enterprise Data Warehouse. This Business Intelligence Asset Base Component is described in Chapter 9. Each of the Key Assessment Features and how to audit them are included in that chapter.

There are individual Audit Scorecards™ for each component of the Business Intelligence Asset Base.

Audit Scorecard™ for the Business Intelligence Asset Base. On the Audit Scorecard shown in 5-D, i.e. for the Business Intelligence Asset

5-F

Audit Scorecard™

Data Integration Platform

	MANAGEMENT SUPPORT	BUSINESS ALIGNMNT	PARTNERSHIP	BUSINESS GOALS	SCALABILITY	INTEGRATION	ADAPT	PERFORMANCE ADABILITY	USER FRIENDLY	COMPREHENSION	QUALITY	VALUE
KEY PERFORMANCE INDICATORS												
Platform Architecture												
Enterprise Architecture												
Data Architecture												
Data Models												
Meta Data												
Security												
Data Marts												
Enterprise Data Warehouse												

Rate each Key Assessment Feature for each of the KPI's. Rating should be 1 to 5, with 5 as hightest rating. See the appropriate chapter for audit and rating guidelines

ASSET BASE

Base, all the summarized scores from each of the component score-cards are entered. This summary Audit Scorecard™, which includes the ratings for all the components, will be used as a starting point to determine the ultimate ranking of the organization. In large part, that ranking will be based on these results. However, there are also other factors which are considered. For more information on how the Level of Maturity for the organization is derived, read Chapter 6.

In summary, the process involves analysis of the overall ratings along with the audit documentation and the opinions and judgments of the auditors. Using all the related audit results, the capability of the organization in creating and management Business Intelligence is then ranked. The ranking is determined by how those results fit within the Business Intelligence audit 'ruler i.e. the Levels of Maturity (described in the previous section.) The Level of Maturity for an organization denotes how well they are able to create and manage Business Intelligence.

5. The Business Intelligence Audit: Resource Materials

5-G

TBIA Business Intelligence Capability Maturity Model'™

Objectives

1. *Identify and Define* **What to Measure**
2. *Create* **Measurement Factors**
3. *Define a* **Measurement Scale**
4. *Define an* **Audit Metholodgy**
5. *Describe How to* **Use the Audit Results**

This book has been written for use as a reference and guide to the auditing of Business Intelligence assets. The objectives have been identified in Figure 5-G. The resource materials which relate to specific objectives are identified in this chapter. The Resource Materials in the book may be referenced to the objectives.

What to Measure: The Business Intelligence Asset Base, the Components and Key Assessment Features are the objects of the Audit.

The overall Business Intelligence Asset Base is described in Chapter 7. The components of the Business Intelligence Asset Base are described in individual chapters which are devoted to each one. In each of these chapters, the component and each of the Key Assessment Features is described in detail. Materials which concern the audit and any information which might assist in understanding and auditing that component is included in the relevant chapter. Following are the references to

the chapters related to the Business Intelligence Components:
- Chapter 9 - The Data Integration Platform
- Chapter 10 - The Analytics Platform
- Chapter 11 - The Business Intelligence Engine
- Chapter 12 - The Technical Infrastructure
- Chapter 13 - The nonTechnical Infrastructure
- Chapter 14 - Data
- Chapter 15 - Meta Data

Chapter 16 is devoted to a discussion regarding the audit of the development process for Business Intelligence applications.

Measurement Factors; Key Performance Indicators have been identified which are used to measure the Key Assessment Features and Components of the Business Intelligence Asset Base. These are described in detail in Chapter 8.

Measurement Scale: The measurement scale which is used in the TBIA Business Intelligence Capability Maturity Model™ is described in Chapter 6. These are the Levels of Maturity which incor-porate current industry best practices and guidelines.

Audit Methodology. Descriptions of the audit process and how to conduct the audit are included in the materials in Chapters 1 through 5. These chapters contain the foundation level materials and include a detailed description and overview of the Business Intelligence Capability Maturity Model, the Audit Process, and audit tools and guidelines.

How to use the Audit Results: The foundation level materials in the first five chapters include reference to the objectives for a Business Intelligence audit and specific uses for the audit results. Chapter 4, in particular, has some specifics which should be reviewed.

6

Levels of Maturity

Chapter Contents

1. Why Levels of Maturity
2. What are they
3. Assessment of Organization
4. Detailed Descriptions

1. Why Levels of Maturity?

Levels of Maturity have been established to provide standards against which to measure how well an organization is accomplishing the creation and management of Business Intelligence assets. These are guidelines which will allow an organization to:

· measure organization performance against industry practices;

· identify and assess weaknesses and strengths;

· assess risks to the organization associated with the current strategies and management practices for their Business Intelligence assets, and

• identify and continue practices which increase the value of Business Intelligence for the organization.

These Levels of Maturity have been created to provide a Measurement Scale to use as an industry model of best practices and guidelines. This Measurement Scale is a ruler which can be used to compare and measure the capabilities of the organization in the creation and management of Business Intelligence assets.

6-A

TBIA Business Intelligence Capability Maturity Model'

Objectives

1. Identify and Define What to Measure
2. Create Measurement Factors
3. Define a Measurement Scale
4. Define an Audit Metholodgy
5. Describe How to Use the Audit Results

2. Levels of Maturity - what are they?

The Levels of Maturity which have been established to provide rating standards for the assessment of the capabilities of an organization in the creation and management of Business Intelligence assets are described in this chapter. Rating the whole of the organization for a Level of Business Intelligence Capability Maturity should be the final step in any audit process. This rating should be the product of a full analysis and detailed audit of the organization Business Intelligence assets. At this final stage of the audit, the audit team should have a relatively clear picture of how effective the organization is in the management of Business Intelligence assets.

Levels of Maturity
Level 1 - Initial
Level 2 - Elementary Integration
Level 3 - Enterprise Effective
Level 4 - Optimized
Level 5 - Leader

6-B

There are five levels of accomplishment for the management of Business Intelligence for an organization. These are:

Level 1 - Initial - the organization is just getting into Business Intelligence - the Business Intelligence arena is characterized by stand alone data marts - with silos of data. The average rating for the Key Performance Indicators is 1 for all components.

Level 2 - Elementary Integration - *more experienced now, the organization can duplicate the basic Business Intelligence technology for new applications, e.g. new data marts. First steps have been made in integration of the data - either federated architectures or an elementary data warehouse, i.e. very early stages. The integration attempts may be enterprise supported or the products of individual business areas. In any case, the integration is fragmented and involves only a few selected data stores. The business Intelligence arena may still be characterized by some stand alone data marts. Key Performance Indicators all are at 2 or 3 or lower.*

Level 3 - Enterprise Effective - *the organization has a centralized data warehouse and is relatively mature in use of Busi-ness Intelligence technologies. Most of the business drivers and goals have been recognized. Key Performance Indicators are 3+.*

Level 4 - Optimized - *Business Intelligence technologies are centered around an enterprise data warehouse, are combined with a mature level of business structures, including standards, as well as fully integrated data and meta data libraries. All the Key Performance Indicators are of recognized importance and Business Intelligence components are rated at 4 or 5.*

Level 5 - Leader *The organization has a comprehensive set of optimized Business Intelligence technologies The organization also has moved into and adopted some set of leading, competitive edge strategies, methods and/or systems.*

There is no Level 0 established for the Levels of Maturity for the organization. In the ratings scale described in Chapter 5, Level 0 indicates the absence of the specific audit subject, i.e. the topic being reviewed and assessed. It is assumed that if there is not even a data mart or some indication of Business Intelligence activity, there will be no reason for any audit. Each of the preceding Levels of Maturity are described in more detail later in this chapter.

3. Organization Assessment

The Level of Maturity for an organization is determined by an audit of all the Business Intelligence assets for the organization. The assessment and rating of these assets is described in Chapters 3, 4 and 5. Each of the remainder of the chapters in the book provides more detailed information about assessment of the Business Intelligence assets and of the individual components of the Business Intelligence Asset Base. Using the results of the audit, along with the notes and clarifications from their work, the audit team should be able to assess the organization as a whole and identify an appropriate Level of Maturity.

The Audit Process

The Business Intelligence Capability Maturity Model identifies

- the definitions and descriptions of all the components of the Business Intelligence Asset Base;
- Key Assessment Features for each component, i.e. what should the auditor look for within and about the component to assist in the assessment process;
- Key Performance Indicators - these are drivers and factors which are specific to Business Intelligence systems and assets. The extent of the presence and integration of the Key Performance Indicators is used to rate the success of the Business Intelligence component (or the whole of the Asset Base).

Each of the Business Intelligence Asset Base components and each of the Key Assessment Features, as practiced within the organization, is identified and analyzed. The Key Performance Indicators (See Chapter 8) plus any other audit notes about the specific compo-nent are used to assess and rate each feature, as well as the overall component. In the same manner, a summation of the component ratings and an overall assessment of the organization are used to determine a Level of Maturity in the creation and management of Business Intelligence assets.

Evolution and Growth

There are some questions management faces when assessing and integrating the results of this audit process and the Level of Maturity findings into an organization strategy.

· How do we use the information?

· Do we make a concerted effort to move to a specific Level of Maturity?

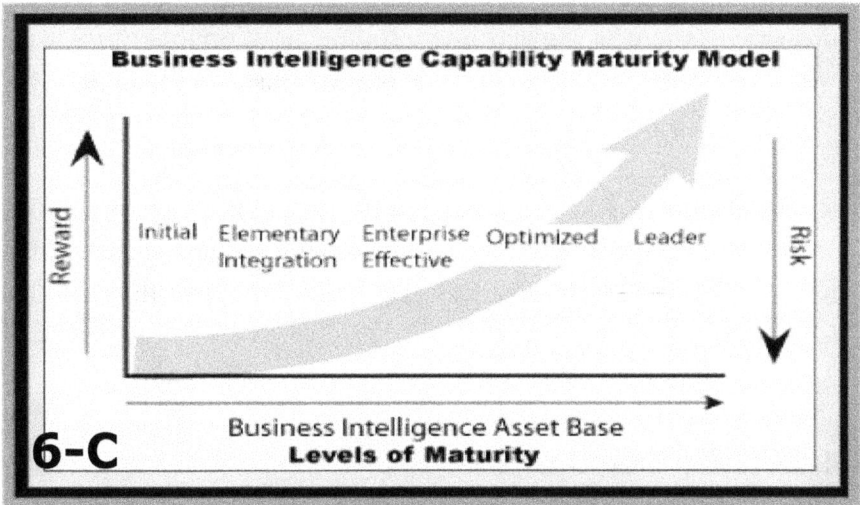

• How critical are all the Key Assessment Features and the Key Performance Indicators and drivers to our organization? Do we need each one? Can we concentrate only on those features and Key Performance Indicator's aligned to our specific needs? What are those specific needs? Management must assess the organization, determine requirements, develop a strategy and plan their audit accordingly.

Impact of Maturity Level

Rewards. One of the deciding factors in making a decision regarding the pursuit of improvement and the level of maturity in management of the Business Intelligence assets is, of course, the resulting benefits. As the organization matures and becomes increasingly more skillful in creating and using Business Intelligence, the rewards from the resulting positive impact to Business Intelligence quality and to the organization effectiveness in the marketplace are correspondingly increased. How much? That is sometimes hard to measure. Is there an impact? There is little question that those firms who are leaders in the management of their Business Intelligence assets are also leaders in their business arenas.

Risk. On another scale entirely lies the question of how much risk an organization incurs by not understanding and using their Business Intelligence assets effectively. How can you assess the risks unless you know what they are?

4. Detailed Descriptions

TBIA BUSINESS INTELLIGENCE CAPABILITY MATURITY MODEL™ Levels of Maturity

These Levels of Maturity described in this chapter satisfy the objectives for a Measurement Scale for the TBIA Business Intelligence Capability Maturity Model™. Each of the Levels of Maturity is defined and described in detail on the following pages. These materials should be used in the Business Intelligence audit process, as well as in the final assessment of the organization.

6-D

Key Performance Indicators

Management support
Business alignment
Business – IT partnership
Business goals-requirements
Integration
Scalability
Adaptability
Performance
Reliability
Ease of Use
Maturity
Scope & Comprehension
Velocity
Quality

Level of Maturity Descriptions

Levels of Maturity will be described on the following pages in terms of the application of the Key Performance Indicators (6-D) to the Business Intelligence Asset Base and the associated components (6-E)

6-E

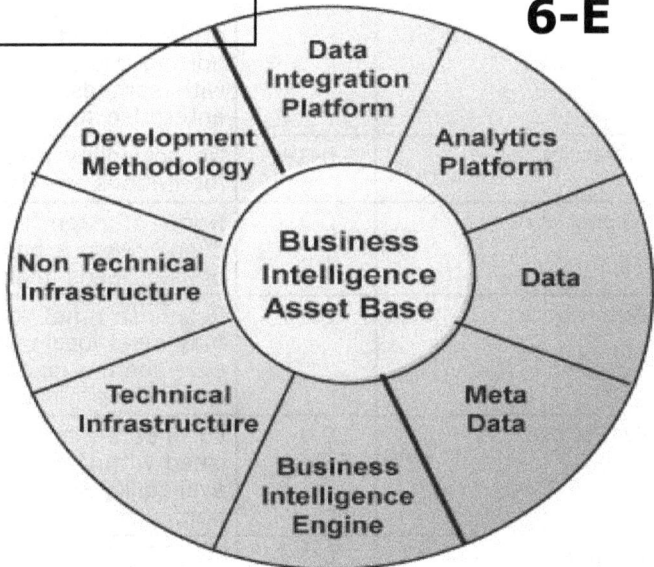

Data Integration Platform
Analytics Platform
Development Methodology
Non Technical Infrastructure
Business Intelligence Asset Base
Data
Technical Infrastructure
Meta Data
Business Intelligence Engine

6-F   Level 1 - Initial

Key Performance Indicator	Rating	Business Intelligance Asset Base (Overall)
Management Support	0-1+	Local Department Management Initiatives. No general enterprise BI understanding and support.
Business Alignment	0-1+	Enterprise Management is not developing BI goals to mathch with the enterprise strategies.
Business-IT Partnership	0-1+	Mainly initiatives are driven in isolation by either business staff or Information Technology staff, working alone.
Business Goals/Requirements	0-1+	The local data marts have departmental goals. If there is an IT initiative - there is little business alignment.
Integration	0-1+	Data is most often in desktop databases eg Microsoft Access, or other isolated platforms. BI reporting and analysis is most often with spreadsheets or local, non-enterprise supported BI tools.
Scalability	0-1+	No scalability - tools and implementations are stand-alone.
Adaptability	0-1+	None System is not in place to even measure how well a variety of user needs might be met.
Performance	0-1+	Response times and other criteria may meet local user needs. However, there is no availability to others in the organizaion.
Ease of Use	0-1+	Local data mart users may be satisfied with their applications. No availability to others in organization.
Comprehension	0-1+	The data marts and/or the data warehouse are very limited in the amount of available data..
Product Quality	0-1+	Data quality is constrained by the sources -- no comparisons with the remainder of the enterprise is possible

Business Intelligence
Capability Maturity Model
Maturity Level 1 - Initial

At the lowest or Initial level of Business Intelligence maturity, we find only the basic structures of data collection, transfer to mainly desk top, local work stations and local types of reporting against the data. The data is fragmented and there is no attempt to use common data across the organization.

The Key Performance Indicators for all the components average between 0 and 1. There is some logic to rating performance and ease of use at a higher level for some of the local data marts. However, because of the very limited availability of data, this is of questionable value to the overall assessment. The most helpful approach appears to be -- make the notes of local opinions and discount these to some extent in the overall assessment.

Following are some notes about the key factors in rating an organization at the Level 1 - Initial stage of Business Intelligence maturity.

The discussion is segmented by component, with wrap-up notes on the over-all asset base.

Enterprise Data Warehouse (Data Integration Platform)

If there are data marts but no Data Integration Platform for the organization or any set of business activities, the organization should be rated at Level 1 - the Initial Level of Business Intelligence maturity. An Enterprise Data Warehouse is not present, nor is there any other platform for integration of multiple data sources. If there is any remnant of a data warehouse, then the organization should be rated at least at a Level 2 Maturity status. For Level 1, there will be isolated data marts which have been developed independently by business groups, usually by department staffs.

Since there is no Enterprise Data Warehouse, none of the Key Performance Indicators, except for the Data Mart will register above 0. In rating the effectiveness of the silo Data Marts, the only Key Per-formance Indicators which should register even a trace of movement for these data marts are for Quality and Value. Certainly the people who designed and developed the data mart may have achieved their goals. They may see the results as highly successful. In fact, the success of these early data marts, i.e. these silos of information, are usually the foundation for the growth of the Business Intelligence efforts within an organization.

Organization Level of Maturity.

If there is no Enterprise Data Warehouse and there is at least one data mart, then the organization should be rated at Level 1 - the Initial Level of Maturity for Business Intelligence effectiveness. There is little tangible benefit in reviewing any other Business Intelligence Asset Base components.

If there are multiple data marts AND there is some attempt at integration, e.g. federated data, then the auditor may wish to investigate a little further. The organization rating may be higher - but that is not likely. Unless there is some enduring foundation for integration, like the Enterprise Data Warehouse, there can be no effective higher level of maturity for Business Intelligence asset management.

There are two factors which should be carefully researched and follow-through may be required. If the organization has elected to use Kimball's architecture for a Data Warehouse - then it is possible there are data marts which appear to be isolated instances, or silos. However, the auditor should look for the integrating features and activities which result in the 'conformed dimensions' of the Kimball Data Warehouse BUS. Only in the very early stages of development, i.e. one or two data marts, should there be any question about the presence of an organization data warehouse. All the other Key Performance Indicators for the Enterprise Data Warehouse should be apparent upon further review. This means there should be rec-ognized management support for the Data Warehouse. There should be at least elementary levels of technical and non technical infrastructures in place, as well as teams of business users and informa-tion technology people who are charged with various responsibilities relative to the data warehouse and integration initiative.

The other case where there is a slight possibility of an invalid Level 1 rating for an organization is when the organization has actually moved on to another para-digm of data collection and use --- i.e. streaming data into an Operational Data Store. Since most of the other components and features should also be working in parallel - this is not a likely audit mistake to make.

6-G Level 2 - Elementary Integration

Key Performance Indicator	Rating	Business Intelligance Asset Base (Overall)
Management Support	1-3	May be a single manager sponsor of a data warehouse Support is spottyand political, at best.
Business Alignment	1-3	Litle alignment of of organization needs and BI strategies and applications.
Business-IT Partnership	1-3	Informagion Technology may be driving ghe data warehouse efforts. Business people may be working in isolation - building their own data marts. Rartw rhis KPI higher if the business community, as well as IT, are involved and support the data warehouse.
Business Goals/ Requirements	1-3	The Business Intelligence application development efforts most likely are the result of and meet specific business requirements.
Integration	1-3	There may be some ambiguity about data warehouse architecture and development.
Scalability	1-3	Infrastructures have most likely been constructed around other requirements than those for the data warehouse. A log of work may still be necessary to make any of the BI sysstems scalable
Adaptability	1-3	At this level, there is no real recognition and acceptance of the risks of change to business requirements and the need for the capability to adapt to that change.
Performance	1-3	In terms of speed of response and other performance measures, the Business Intellligence systemsmost likely do not have defined Service Level Agreements with the users Response times and even definition of what those response times should be are not necessarily identified or successfully met.
Ease of Use	1-3	Most likely there are still multiple tools and the design and ease of use of the analytics is not consistent across the tools and the user community.
Comprehension	1-3	Individual BI applications may include all that the business user wishes -howeverk the Data Warehouse is most likely sketchy and contains only a small subset of the information required for the organization decision support needs.
Product Quality	1-3	Some data is trusted by some of the users - however there is most likely not a general feeling of trust and faith in the data across the organization.
Value to Cost	1-3	Because of the nature of and the continuing existence of siloed data marts and the sstart up costs associated with the Enterprie Data Warehouse, the effective cost to value received by the organization at this stage of maturity is **very high.**

Business Intelligence
Capability Maturity Model
Maturity Level 2
Elementary Integration

Maturity Level 2 is characterized by the presence of a rudimentary Enterprise Data Warehouse along with departmental or group data marts which remain essentially silos of data. Each of the Business Intelligence Asset Base Components should have been rated for each Key Performance Indicator and the average of the ratings are between 1+ and 2.

Enterprise Data Warehouse. Some effort should be in process toward a full enterprise level data integration platform via Extract, Transform, Load (ETL) tools, along with standards and infrastructures. There may still be isolated data marts which are silos of data. Some of the data marts, however, should be associated and integrated into the Enterprise Data Warehouse structures.

Analytics Platform. There are most likely a number of Analytic -Business Intelligence toolsets which are departmental purchases, with department level responsibility. There may or may not be enterprise selected and supported software and infrastructures.

Data. Quality of data is questionable, at best. There may be some sat-isfaction at the local (departmental) level, but the data at the enterprise level cannot be trusted without extensive, manual intervention.

Business Intelligence Engine. The basic technical infrastructure should be in place for Extract, Transform and Load (ETL) activities-However, the development, non technical infrastructures, and comprehension may be sketchy.

Technical Infrastructure. The Technical Infrastructure includes all the hardware, communications structures, networks, middleware, and tools. Since an Enterprise Data Warehouse exists, most of the key ingredients should be in place. However, because of application and effectiveness, the Key Performance Indicators will only range between 0 and 2.

nonTechnical Infrastructure. The standards, procedures, training & communications and other Key Assessment Features within the nonTechnical Infrastructure may or may not be present. If present, the average rating will be 0 - 2+.

Development Methodology. Development is still most likely to be in separated areas or departments across the organization. There may be some attempts at bringing the efforts into a single, enterprise sup¬ported layer of activities. Ratings for some individual development efforts may vary. However, unless there is an enterprise supported and governed development platform, then this component should be rated no higher than a Level 2.

BUSINESS INTELLIGENCE ASSET BASE - OVERALL

Overall - the final rating of the Business Intelligence Asset Base for the organization will average out to a Level 2. If there are anomalies and some spikes either way, then these areas should be explored in a little more depth. There may be some information which is missing. Auditors should always use their own on-site judgement in rating the maturity of the organization. These guidelines and the detailed information which is included in the remainder of the book are simply that - guidelines.

6-G Level 3 - Enterprise Effective

Key Performance Indicator	Rating	Business Intelligance Asset Base (Overall)
Management Support	2-4	Management support may be strong in some areas - but there may still be some political hurdles to full commitment & support for the Business Inteligence efforts.
Business Alignment	2-4	Alignment of business strategies, plans and requirements may be sketchy and not clearly defined.
Business-IT Partnership	2-4	Business and Information Technology resources may work together on most aspects of Business Intelligence.
Business Goals/ Requirements	2-4	Business Intelligence application development efforts will most often result from and meet specific business requirements.
Integration	2-4	There is an accepted architecture and models for the integration of data. There may not be a strong, enterprise-mandated and governed data integration program across the organization and for new development.
Scalability	2-4	Infrasructures, both for the data integrationn platform and the analytical platform are designed, architected and implemented to satisfy the requirements for changes in volumes and other requirements of the users, data and automated tools There may be areas which are not copliant and need upgrade.
Adaptability	2-4	In many cases, at this level, there is no real recognition and acceptance of the risks of change to business requirements and the need for the capability to adapt to that change.
Performance	2-4	In terms of speed of response and other performance measures, the Business Intelligence systems may have defined Service Level Agreements with the users. Meeting those agreeents or satifying the needs of the users may not be consistently successful. Data is 'historic' in nature, i.e. not real time or 'near real' time.
Ease of Use	2-4	Most likely there are still multiple BI Analtical tools and the design and ease of use of the analytics is not consistent across the tools and the user community. .
Comprehension	2-4	Individual BI applications may include all that the business user wishes - however, the Data Warehouse is most likely sketch and contains only a small subset of the information required for the organization decision support needs.
Product Quality	2-4	Some data is trusted by some users --however, there is most likely not a general feeling of trust and faith in the data across the organization.
Value to Cost	2-4	Because of the nature of some of the continuing existence of siloed data marts and start up costs associated with the Enterprise Data Warehouse, the effective cost to value received by the organization at this stage of maturity is **medium to high**.

Business Intelligence
Capability Maturity Model
Maturity Level 3
Enterprise Effective

Maturity Level 3 is characterized by the existence of an enterprise supported Data Warehouse and Analytics Platform. There should be no recognized non integrated silos of data, i.e. data marts which are not part of the established Business Intelligence platforms. If there are, then the organization should be rated at Maturity Level 2. There is a reasonable level of management support and the users are relatively satisfied with the business intelligence being generated. Use of the Data Warehouse still needs strong marketing efforts to reach the necessary cross-enterprise body of users. Trust in the quality of the data is fair - but should be improving as programs and governance are put in place. There are definitely improvements which need to be made in areas like the technical and non technical infrastructures, meta data and perhaps, such items as performance and Service Level Agreements. The organization is rated at a Level 3 Maturity because of the weakness in some of these, or other crucial areas of interest. There may even be some fuzziness related to the Enterprise Data Warehouse architectures, models and development strategies. With two major industry accepted architectures, it is sometimes difficult for an organization to find agreement in the ranks for one or the other. Each of the Business Intelligence Asset Base Components should have been rated for each Key Performance Indicator and the average of the ratings should be 3-+/-. Since a major characteristic of this Maturity Level is a wide variation in the component structures and capabilities - the ratings for the Key Assessment Features and the associated Key Performance Indicators may not be uniform. Some may be very highly rated - some relatively low.

Enterprise Data Warehouse. The Enterprise Data Warehouse should be fully realized with ETL tools, standards and infrastructures. The capabilities may be weak in some areas, stronger in others. There should no longer be any isolated data marts which are silos of data. If there are, then the organization should be rated at Maturity Level 2.

Analytics Platform. User interface is primarily with enterprise supported analytics tools. The analytics are mostly 'out-of-the-box' query, standard reporting, and OLAP. There are Information Technology developers who work with the business users in developing new and enhanced Business Intelligence applications.

Data. Quality of data is fair to good. Cleansing and integration efforts have created a credible library of information. There may or may not be solid programs for data stewardship and data certification.

Meta data. Quality and comprehension of meta data is sketchy, with no enterprise integrating methods, like an Enterprise Meta Data Repository.

Business Intelligence Engine. The basic technical infrastructure and software should be in place for Extract, Transform and Load (ETL) activities. However, the development, non technical infrastructures, and comprehension may be sketchy.

Technical Infrastructure. The Technical Infrastructure includes, of course, all the hardware, communications structures, networks, middleware, and tools. Since an Enterprise Data Warehouse exists, most of the key ingredients should be in place. Selected features may not be geared to Business Intelligence requirements - and there may be scalability, adaptability, and performance issues.

nonTechnical Infrastructure. There should be a relatively effective level of cohesion and support. However, the standards, procedures, training & communications and other Key Assessment Features within the nonTechnical Infrastructure may or may not be present. Development Methodology. Development is still most likely occurring in separated departments across the organization. There may be some attempts at bringing the efforts into a single, enterprise supported layer of operations. Ratings for individual development efforts may vary.

BUSINESS INTELLIGENCE ASSET BASE - OVERALL
Overall - the final rating of the Business Intelligence Asset Base for the organization will average out to a Level 3. The determining factors are - a working Enterprise Data Warehouse and Analytics Platform which satisfy the needs at some level for the Business Intelligence users. There are NO isolated data marts with silos of data. Other fea¬tures and Key Performance Indicators may be spotty - high or low.

6-I Level 4 - Optimized

Key Performance Indicator	Rating	Business Intelligance Asset Base (Overall)
Management Support	3-5	Management is strongly supportive of their Business Intelligence efforts.
Business Alignment	3-5	Business Intelligence Assets, architectures and plans are aligned to business strategy and tactical plans.
Business-IT Partnership	3-5	Business and Informqtion Technology resoures work closely on all aspecdts of Business Intellience. .
Business Goals/ Requirements	3-5	Priorities, plans and development are focused on the satisfaction of business goals and requirements.
Integration	3-5	There is a strong, clearly defined program and accepted arhitectures and models for the integration of data.
Scalability	3-5	Infrastructures, both for the data integration platform and the analytical platform are designed, architected and implemented to satisfy the requirements for changes in volumes and other requirements of the users, data, and automated tools.
Adaptability	3-5	The systems, infrastructures and architectures are designed to ensure that changes in business requirements can be met with satisfactory Business Intelligence.
Performance	3-5	In terms of speed of response and other performance measures, the Businss Intelligence systems have defined Service Level Agreements with the users and meet those agreements. Some 'near real time' applications data may be available - but generally the data is not available on a 'real time' bais - and is 'historical' in nature.
Ease of Use	3-5	Analytical tools are well designed to allow 'guided analytics'. Business users can assist in design and development efforts through the facilitation of 'user friendly' data models and tools.
Comprehension	3-5	Data Warehouse includes or there are plans for all the information which the organization requires in the Business Intelligence Asset Base.
Product Quality	3-5	Information is trusted by all the users in the system. Where there are questions, there are clearldy defined procedures for questioning and changing. Data stewards are identified for all data within the system. Data is certified by the system and full audit meta data is maintained.
Value to Cost	3-5	Emphasis is on using Business Intelligence for the best decision making possible - but management will be aware of the prioritizing based on their goals and requirements and getting th most for the resources expended. Cost to value is **fair to low.**

Business Intelligence
Capability Maturity Model
Maturity Level 4
Optimized

An organization with a maturity level of 4 is creating and using Business Intelligence in a manner which provides excellent business decision support. The management is progressive in their support and creative utilization of Business Intelligence and it shows in their placement in their market environment. The primary differences between the Business Intelligence Asset Base for the organization at a Maturity Level of 4 and Maturity Level 5 are the 'leading edge' features - e.g. real time/right time data; integration of unstructured data; and perhaps, a stronger universal access mechanism and search engine.

Each of the Business Intelligence Asset Base Components should have been rated for each Key Performance Indicator and the average of the ratings should be between 3 and 5.

Enterprise Data Warehouse. There is a fully realized data warehouse. The architecture is clearly defined and understood. Management support is strong and politics do not interfere with operations. Business Users and Information Technology specialists are equally involved and have joint ownership responsibilities. There are joint working teams for integration and architecture, as well as other general cross-organization issues. All data marts are integrated into the Enterprise Data Warehouse architecture and data structures.

Analytics Platform. There are analytical toolsets which have been chosen and/or developed and are supported at the enterprise level. These tools satisfy the wide variety of user requirements, and where there are questions or issues, these are resolved at the enterprise level. The analytics platform offers tools which guide both the new user and the 'power' user through the necessary Business Intelligence analytics - at the appropriate level of understanding and pace.

Data. Quality of data is unquestioned and trusted by everyone in the organization. There are mandated data reviews, Business Intelligence application reviews, data stewardship programs, and full data certification requirement for all data.

Meta data. Quality and comprehension of meta data is excellent. There may be an automated and online enterprise meta data repository, which integrates all meta data from Business Intelligence tools. If present, this library of information about the data may also feature interactive user creation and update of the meta data and 'near real time' update of all models, toolset information and databases. If an enterprise meta data repository is not fully realized, the organization may still be rated at a Level 4. Use your judgement about how well the current organization meta data requirements are being met.

Business Intelligence Engine. Extract, Transform and Load (ETL) activities have been expanded to provide for all the requirements for a fully integrated information platform. Data is extracted from multiple data sources and quickly moved through the transformation and integration in the staging areas and processes and into a fully integrated information presentation library. Access to the data is made flexible and easy to use by the appropriate tools and architectures. At the Optimized level of maturity, these Business Intelligence Engines may interface with not only standard data sources. There may also be some recognition and interface with a much broader range of data services within an Service Oriented Architecture.

Technical Infrastructure. The Technical Infrastructure includes all the hardware, middleware, networks, and tools necessary to a well conceived and designed Business Intelligence arena. The hardware, middleware and software have been chosen for performance and to meet the specific requirements of the organization. The infrastructure is scalable and adaptable and has been specifically designed and is maintained with those features in mind. The infrastructures may be adapted to fit in to a larger enterprise architectural arena of a Service Oriented Architecture of the progressive organization.

nonTechnical Infrastructure. The standards, procedures, training & communications and other Key Assessment Features within the nonTechnical Infrastructure are all present and can be rated at least at a level 4. All those which are required for a well established and optimized Business Intelligence environment are in place and are carefully monitored to meet any new or changing requirements.

Development Methodology. There is a well established methodology for the development and enhancement of Business Intelligence data and analytics. Any development activity is mandated to follow the established processes and there is governance, including review and follow-up to ensure that all criteria are met. The development is mainly iterative, with predevelopment testing of data, business rules, and analytics to reduce costs and enhance the chances of success.

BUSINESS INTELLIGENCE ASSET BASE - OVERALL Overall - This organization has optimized its creation and utilization of Business Intelligence for decision support activities and action and has proven successful in their market arena.

6-J   Level 5 - Leader

Key Performance Indicator	Rating	Business Intelligance Asset Base (Overall)
Management Support	4-5	Management is aggressively seeking the best in business intelligence and is willing to take risks and expend resources.
Business Alignment	4-5	Business Intelligence assets, architectures, and plans are closely aligned to business strategy and tactical plans.
Business-IT Partnership	4-5	Business and Information Technology resources work very closely on all aspects of Business Intelligence. .
Business Goals/ Requirements	4-5	Priorities, plans and development are all focused on the satisfaction of business goals and requirements.
Integration	4-5	All possible tools, architectures, and strategies are implemented in the search and satisfactio of the requirements for the data and other forms of Business Intelligence integration. Both structured and unstructured data are included and seamlessly architected.
Scalability	4-5	Infrasatructures - both for the data integration platform and the analytical platform- are designed, architected and implemented to satisfy the requirements for fast changes in volumes and other requirements of the users, data and automated tools.
Adaptability	4-5	Management ensures that from infrastructures and hardware to human resources, the company is ready to recognize and react to any new threats or opportunities.
Performance	4-5	Sets and meets Service Level Agreements. In terms of speed of response, the Business Intelligence systems meet both the historic information requirements as well as the 'near real time' requirements.
Ease of Use	4-5	Analytical tools are well designed to allow 'guided analytics'. Users can assist in designe and development efforts through facilitation of 'user friendly' data models and tools. Universal access to the BI, both structured and unstructured data, throuogh a portal/web delivery. Powerful search engine in use. Automated library and comprehensive metadata.
Comprehension	4-5	All information requirements are available or planned. Structured and unstructured information is complete and accessible.
Product Quality	4-5	Information is trusted by all users. Clearly defined procedures for questions and changes. Data certification and stewardship programs in place. Full audit meta data in place.
Value to Cost	4-5	Emphasis is on using BI for the best decision making possible. Management is aware of the need for prioritizing and getting the most for resources expended. Low cost to value.

Business Intelligence
Capability Maturity Model
Maturity Level 5
Leader

Maturity Level 5 shows the aggressive action of management in the utilization of Business Intelligence for decision making within the organization. Not only have they ensured an Optimized environment, they have pushed forward to a leadership position. This organization now has:

· a fully realized Enterprise Data Warehouse;

· an Enterprise Analytics Platform which highlights guided analytical Business Intelligence access and fol¬low through;

· a new paradigm of Business Intelligence activity for real time and 'near real' time (i.e. right time) accessibility to operational data, as required;

· an information base which includes both structured and unstructured data, which has been integrated into a seam-less library;

universal access, through an enterprise portal or similar technology;

· a search engine which matches the best of the web engines;

· designed to fit into an enterprise Service Oriented Architecture (SOA), rather than historic, stand-alone data warehouse.

Each of the Business Intelligence Asset Base Components should have been rated for each of the Key Performance Indicators and t politics does not interfere with operations. Business Users and Information Technology specialists are equally involved and have joint ownership responsibilities. There are joint working teams for integration and architecture, as well as other general cross-organization issues. All data marts are integrated into the information library architecture and data structures.

Analytics Platform. There are analytical toolsets which have been chosen and/or developed and are supported at the organization level. These tools satisfy the wide variety of user requirements; and where there are questions or issues, these are resolved at the enterprise level. The analytics platform offers tools which guide both the new user and the 'power' user through the necessary Business Intelligence analytics - at the appropriate level of understanding and pace.

Data. Quality of data is unquestioned and trusted by everyone in the organization. There are mandated data reviews, Business Intelligence application reviews, data stewardship programs, and a full data certification program for all data.

Meta data. Quality and comprehension of meta data is excellent. There may be an automated and online enterprise meta data repository, which integrates all meta data from Business Intelligence tools. This is the level of Business Intelligence maturity where such an enterprise library of meta data is most likely to be found. This library of information about the data may also include interactive user creation and update of the meta data and 'near real time' update of all models, toolset information and databases.

Business Intelligence Engine. Extract, Transform and Load (ETL) activities have been expanded to provide for all the requirements of a fully integrated information platform. Data is extracted from multiple data sources and quickly moved through the transformation and integration in the staging areas and into a fully integrated in¬formation presentation library. There may also be some recognition and interface with a much broader range of data services within an Service Oriented Architecture.

Technical Infrastructure. The Technical Infrastructure includes all the hardware, middleware, networks, and tools necessary to a well conceived and designed Business Intelligence arena. The database management systems have been chosen for performance and to meet the specific requirements of the organization. The infrastructure is scalable and adaptable and has been specifically designed and is maintained with those features in mind. The infrastructures may be adapted to fit in to a larger enterprise architectural arena of a Service Oriented Architecture of the progressive organization.

nonTechnical Infrastructure. The standards, procedures, training & communications and other Key Assessment Features within the nonTechnical Infrastructure are all present and can be rated at least at a level 4. All those which are required for a well established and optimized Business Intelligence environment are in place and carefully monitored to meet any new or changing requirements.

Development Methodology. There is a well established methodology for the development and enhancement of Business Intelligence Any development activity is mandated to follow the established processes and there is governance, including review and follow-up, to ensure that all criteria are met. The development is mainly iterative, with predevelopment testing of data, business rules, and analytics to reduce costs and enhance the changes of success.

BUSINESS INTELLIGENCE ASSET BASE - OVERALL
Overall - This organization is a leader in the creation and use of Business Intelligence for decision support activities and action and has proven their success in their market arena.

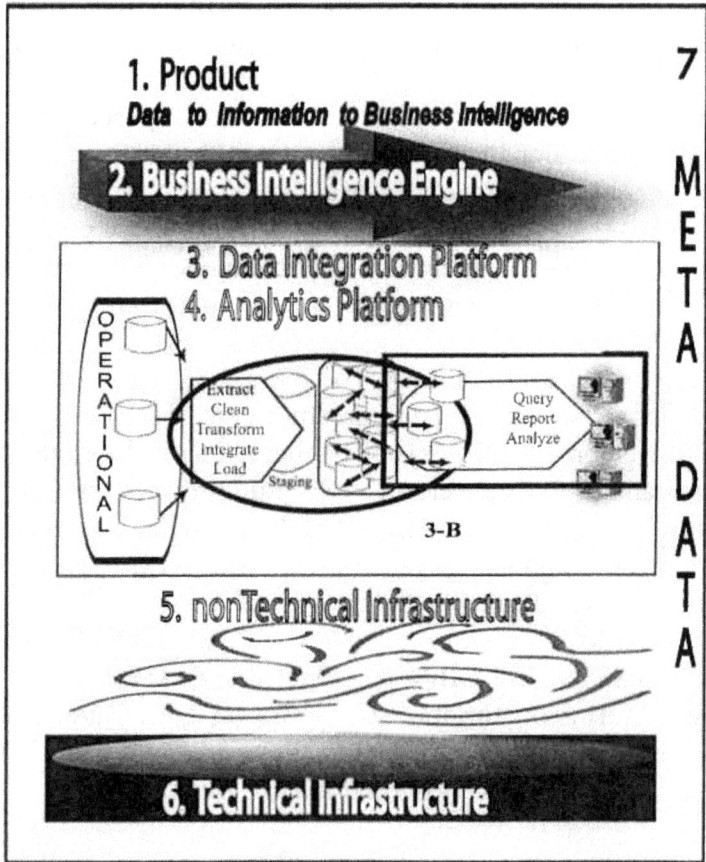

CHAPTER 7

Business Intelligence Asset Base

Chapter Contents

1. Objectives
2. Business Intelligence Assets
3. Business Intelligence Asset Base Components
4. Business Intelligence Audit Wheel
5. Business Intelligence Asset Base Audit Scorecard

1. Objectives

It is important to identify, define and describe the exact nature and all the parts which are included in the Business Intelligence assets for an organization. There is no way to study and analyze the assets if they cannot be defined. The objective of this chapter is to provide an overview and complete picture of the Business Intelligence Asset Base.

The focus is on the overall Business Intelligence Asset Base, and the architectures, with a brief introduction to each of the Business Intelligence components. Each of the components will be further described and discussed in later chapters.

In satisfying Objective 1 of the TBIA Business Intelligence Capabiity Maturity Model™, two primary goals have been defined.

1. To layout a blueprint of the Business Intelligence Asset Base. To identify and describe the Business Intelligence assets, as a whole, and to identify, define and draw the relationships among the Business Intelligence parts.

2. To provide detailed information about each component of the Business Intelligence Asset Base. This detailed information and further descriptions are focused on the first and second level Business Intelligence Audit process.

7-A
TBIA Business Intelligence Capability Maturity Model™
Objectives

1. **Identify and Define What to Measure**
2. **Create Measurement Factors**
3. **Define a Measurement Scale**
4. **Define an Audit Metholodgy**
5. **Describe How to Use the Audit Results**

This chapter is focused on the first of these goals. The later chapters devoted to each component address the second goal and will include more details and audit guidelines for each part of the Business Intelligence Asset Base.

Restating the obvious. Auditing Business Intelligence is critical to the successful oversight and management of Business Intelligence assets. The first step in any audit process is to understand the Business Intelligence Asset Base. What are Business Intelligence assets? How can we estimate return on investment or evaluate risk factors without a clear picture of the Business Intelligence assets? Business Intelligence assessment demands that we, first of all, understand what we are trying to review. We need an inventory and description of all the parts and pieces which comprise Business Intelligence for the organization. From this inventory and understanding, we can begin to formulate a strategy, and to plan for an audit of these 'parts and pieces' and how they fit together. How well or how badly the constructs, architectures and components within the Business Intelligence apparatus work is the subject of the audit.

2. The Business Intelligence Asset Base

The parts of Business Intelligence are numerous and complex. These assets are spread like a spider web throughout the organization. Perhaps the simplest way to understand the full nature of Business Intelligence is to step back and look at the whole picture. There are three levels which comprise the Business Intelligence Asset Base.

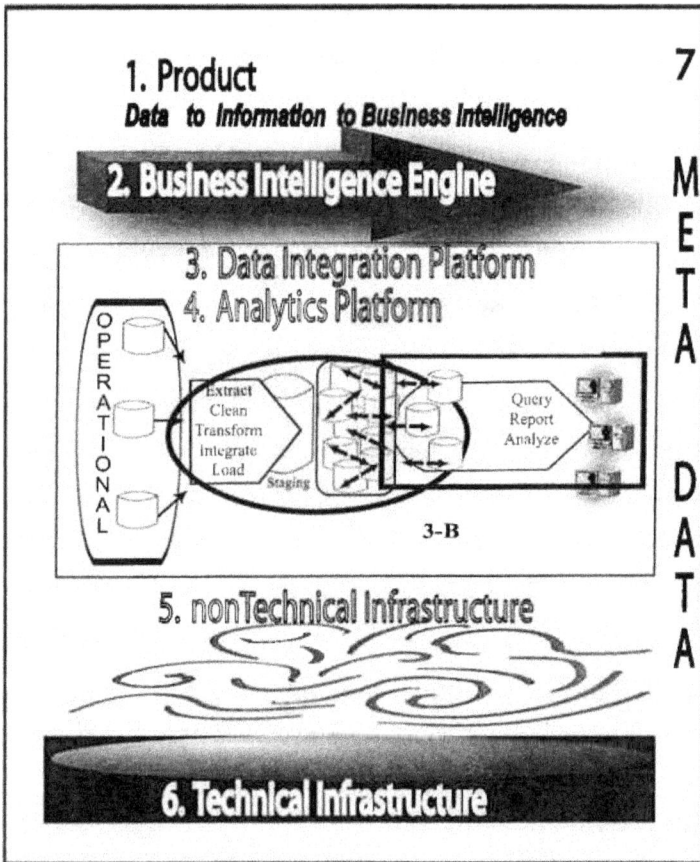

1. Product
Data to Information to Business Intelligence

2. Business Intelligence Engine

3. Data Integration Platform
4. Analytics Platform

OPERATIONAL

Extract
Clean
Transform
Integrate
Load
Staging

Query
Report
Analyze

3-B

5. nonTechnical Infrastructure

6. Technical Infrastructure

7
M
E
T
A
D
A
T
A

7-B The Business Intelligence Asset Base

1. Level 1 — the platform architectures. These are the Data Integration Platform and the Analytical Platform.

2. Level 2 — the nonTechnical Infrastructure. This is the whole set of guidelines, standards, training and communications, gov-er-nance and a myriad of other topics and constructs which provide the glue and makes for successful Business Intelligence.

3. Level 3 — the Technical Infrastructure. The hardware, tool sets, middleware, communications, data base management systems, meta data management systems and other such tangible constructs and components.

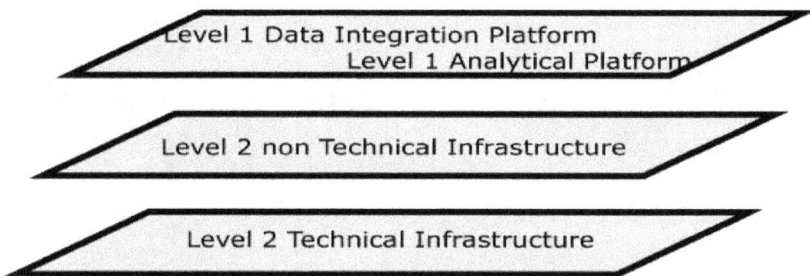

Level 1 Data Integration Platform
Level 1 Analytical Platform

Level 2 non Technical Infrastructure

Level 2 Technical Infrastructure

7-C Levels of Business Intelligence Architecture

In addition to these three levels of the Business Intelligence architecture foundation, there are several other components which are essential parts of the Business Intelligence Asset Base. The Business Intelligence Engine is the driving force which collects, transforms, and moves the product across the Business Intelligence platforms and infrastructures. The Business Intelligence Engine incorporates and expands upon those constructs which are usually labeled Extract, Transform, and Load. The Business Intelligence Product is considered, for audit purposes, to begin with the 'raw' data and moves through several transformations to Information and then to Business Intelligence.

The Development Methodology for creating the Business Intelligence Assets is also a key part of the Business Intelligence Asset Base. How these assets are planned, designed and developed shapes the entire nature and the contents of the Business Intelligence Asset Base. Understanding and assessing the Development Methodology is crucial to understanding and realizing the Business Intelligence potential and capacity within an organization.

3. The Business Intelligence Asset Base Components

The Platform Architectures.

The Data Integration Platform

In most of today's more mature organizations, the data integration platform is, in fact, the Enterprise Data Warehouse. The Enterprise Data Warehouse provides the architecture for collection and integration of data from multiple sources, and the establishment of a library of business information which is a 'single source of truth' for the organization. There are other integration methods, like federation of data, i.e. which refers to the virtual integration of multiple data sources. However, the Data Integration Platform is most often an Enterprise Data Warehouse. The primary roles of the Data Integration Platform are to collect the 'raw' product, Data, and to transform and integrate it into a unified and uniform library of quality Information.

7-D Platform Architectures

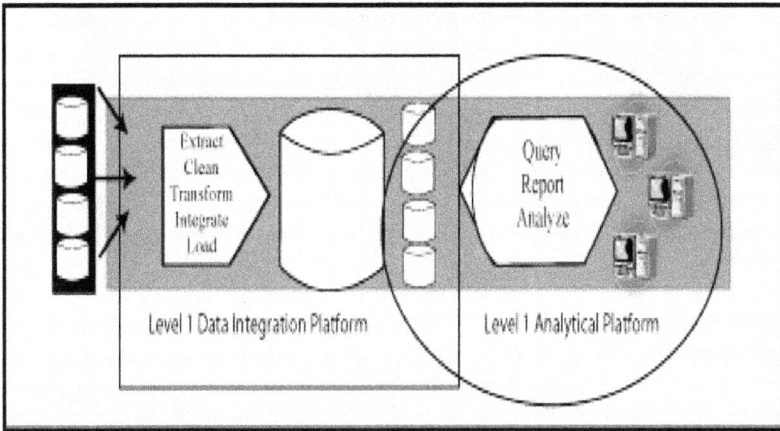

The Analytics Platform

The Analytics Platform provides the user access and interface to the Business Information. This includes all the analytical tools, deliv¬ery mechanisms, formatting, and user interface. The presentation library of the Enterprise Data Warehouse is where all the cleansed, translated, unified information is stored. The Analytics Platform provides access to this information.

The query, reporting, and analysis of the data and the interface with the end users is the province of a myriad number of vendors and toolsets. There are several primary categories for these business intelligence end products.

The tools and activities may be categorized as
  · query and reporting
  · on line analysis processing (OLAP) along with the dif-ferent forms of the data models and processing which support varia-

tions - i.e. relational on line analysis processing (ROLAP); multidimensional on line analysis processing (MOLAP).

· data mining and statistical analysis
· forecasting and simulation

The Product

The end product is Business Intelligence. This is Business Information which has been integrated with human resources or automated systems in order to better understand and manage the organization. Accurate information, which is complete, timely, and easily accessible can make the difference in success or failure for any organization.

Data is the initial, i.e. 'raw', product. Data is collected from a myriad different sources and is gathered into a library within the Data Integration Platform That data is the basis for the business information and the final Business Intelligence product which can be used by the organization to understand, manage and plan for the operations of the business. A distinction is made here between business information and Business Intelligence. In much of the current industry language, the two terms are synonymous or blurred. However, there continue to be some valid reasons for remembering the difference. Business Information is the passive form. It is created and exists in isolation within the computer or whatever the commu-nications form. Business Intelligence requires the interface with the mind of a human or a computer system which has been programmed to accept and use the business information and provides automated interface and response.

Note: Security of the product is addressed as a primary Key Assessment Feature for Data and other Business Intelligence Asset Base Components.

The nonTechnical Infrastructure

The secondary layer in this virtual Business Intelligence blueprint includes the infrastructures which support and provide the cohesion for the Data Integration Platform and the Analytics Platform. The nonTechnical Infrastructure layer is composed of all the 'soft' or `intangible' glue components. This includes features and functions such as standards, guidelines, processes, initiative and governance.

These are the components which overlay and provide the cross organization framework for Business Intelligence. The non technical components of the Business Intelligence Asset Base are defined as anything necessary to the operations and success of the Business Intelligence for an organization which can NOT be included in any of the other Business Intelligence Asset Base components. As noted, this includes the standards, policies, procedures, and special initiatives and programs which are layered and integrated into the structure of the Business Intelligence Asset Base.

The Technical Infrastructure

The Technical Infrastructure includes Hardware, Middleware, Database Management Systems, Meta Data Management Systems, Networks and communications plus all the software and other tools. This Technical Infrastructure provides the architectural base and support for both the Data Integration Platform and the Analytics Platform.

Some of the important characteristics of the Technical Infrastructure are:

· How well is it designed and built to match the requirements for Business Intelligence for the organization, and
· Does it meet the standards described by the Business Intelligence Key Performance Indicators.

The Business Engine

This is the construct used in the Business Intelligence Capability Maturity Model to describe and clarify the collection, transformation, and movement of data across the various parts of the Business Intelligence Asset Base. This Business Intelligence Engine includes all of the Extract, Transform and Load (ETL) activities and expands on the functions and features. This Business Intelligence Engine also includes the access and delivery of the integrated information into the hands of the final users.

Meta Data

Meta data is Information about Data. Meta Data is a part of several components within the Business Intelligence Asset Base. The prod-uct, the infrastructures, the Business Engine - all have meta data aspects and these Business Intelligence Asset Base components include a meta data Key Assessment Feature. Meta Data is reviewed during any audit of those components. However, Meta Data is also treated within the Business Intelligence Capability Maturity Model as a separate and unique component. The major reason for this is to

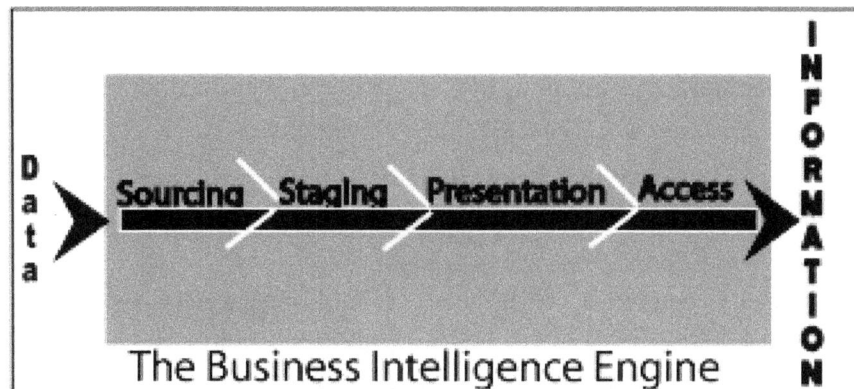

ensure that the importance and place for meta data is under-**7-E**
stood and documented. Meta Data is all the information about
DATA - both technical and business. In fact, without a considerable
amount of Meta Data, there can be no transformation of Data into
Business Information and Business Intelligence. Therefore, the importance of Meta Data needs to be highlighted. A second reason for
concern and for special treatment of Meta Data is that it is so easy to
overlook it. For decades, information systems developers have considered 'documentation', which is to a great extent, what Meta Data
represents, to be on the lowest rung of their priority lists. The job of
documentation most often was assigned to the lowest ranking team
members and then usually only as a 'wrap-up' assignment for the
project. The current frequently poor state of the Meta Data within an
organization is the result of these decades of neglect.

Meta Data may be divided into two categories:
- · Business Meta Data - all the definitions and information necessary to understand the Business Language of the organization;

and

· Technical Meta Data - all the information necessary to understand the underlying data structures and data movement within and across the Business Intelligence Asset Base.

Development Methodology

This is the component of the Business Intelligence Asset Base which includes all the processes, guidelines, standards and governing rules and characteristics used in creating the Business Intelligence systems and information for the organization. Following a consistent and tested set of processes and methods is important in successfully and consistently providing top value for the expenditures made by the organization. It is important that the guides and standards for development are in place and that they are followed in every case. That means that there should be some check points and governance inherent is the development process. A well designed Development Methodology is of critical importance in creating the assets and ultimately the success of Business Intelligence for an organization.

Author's Note

These Business Intelligence Asset Base Components are further divided into Key Assessment Features. Each of the chapters for individual Business Intelligence Components detail and describe these Key Assessment Features. There may be some topics which the reader would expect to see as a component. In most cases, expect to find these as Key Assessment Features of specific Business In¬telligence Components. Governance and Security might very well fit as a key Business Intelligence component. Just like Meta Data this topic is an integrated part of many of the primary components and could very well stand alone. Please let the author know through our website if you feel strongly about this or other subjects for a revised book.
www.redstone360.com

4. The Audit Wheel™
for Business Intelligence Assets

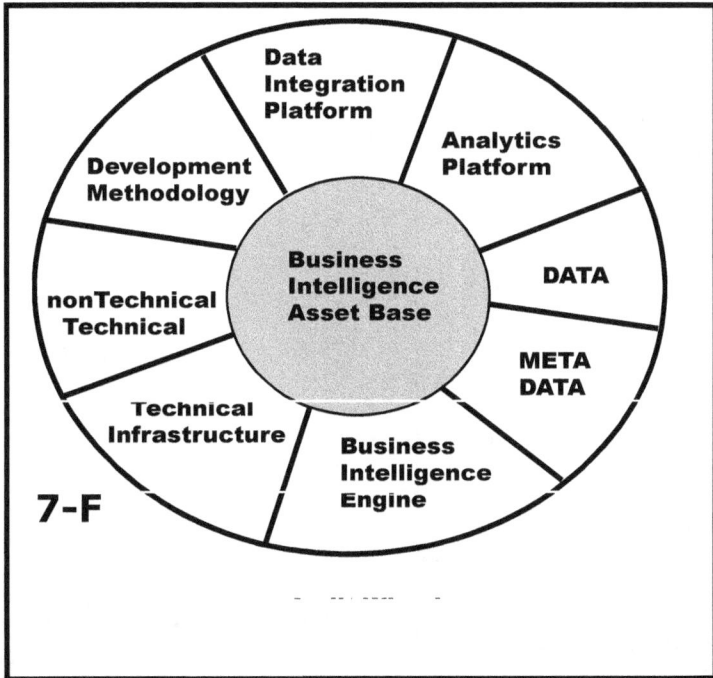

All the Business Intelligence Asset Base components have been incorporated into the Audit Wheel™ shown in 7-F. This chart and other derivative charts for each component will be used in the later chapters in this book which describe the components in more detail. Each of the components of the Business Intelligence Asset Base are subdivided further into first level parts, called Key Assessment Features, in those chapters. Those component parts provide the initial focus of any Business Intelligence audit for the organization.

5. The Audit Scorecard ™ for Business Intelligence Assets

ASSET BASE

Rate each Component of the Business Intelligence Asset Base. This rating should reflect and summarize the detailed rating given for the Key Assessment Features for that Component. Use the Component Ratings to derive the Overall Rating for the Asset Base. Ratings should be 1 - 5, with 5 as highest rating.	KEY PERFORMANCE INDICATORS											
	Mangment Support	BUSINESS ALGNMNT	PARTNERSHIP	Business Goals	Scalability	INTEGRATION	ADAPTABILITY	PERFORMANCE	USER FRIENDLY	COMPREHENSION	QUALITY	VALUE
Data Integration Platform (Enterprise Data Warehouse)												
Analytics Platform												
Data												
Meta Data												
Technical Infrastructure												
NonTechnical Infrastructure												
Business Intelligence Engine												
Development Methodology												
Business Intelligence ASSET BASE												

This is the Audit Scorecard™ for the overall Business Intelligence Asset Base. (See Chapters 1- 5 and later chapters.) This is a form which would include the summarized audit ratings for the overall Business Intelligence Asset Base.

CHAPTER 8

Key Performance Indicators

Chapter Contents

1. Definitions and Use

2. Key Pereformance Indicators

1. Definition and Use

Key Performance Indicators are important characteristics inherent in Business Intelligence assets. Those included in this chapter have been selected as measurement factors which are to be used in the audit process for Business Intelligence, i.e. as part of the Business Intelligence Capability Maturity Model. (see Chapters 3, 4, and 5) These Measurement Factors are used in a Business Intelligence audit in a manner similar to which we might use height as a measurement factor for an object or person. Thus, feet and inches would be the scale or ruler for measurement; and height is the measurement factor. These Key Performance Indicators are also business drivers and objectives used in the creation of the Business Intelligence Asset Base for an organization. Key Performance Indicators, are primary factors which drive the management of Business Intelligence within the organization. These Key Performance Indicators impact the development, creation and usefulness of the business information produced by an organization.

Objectives. The Key Performance Indicators satisfy the objective identified for the Business Intelligence Capability Maturity Model for the creation of Measurement Factors. These Measurement Factors are used to determine the level of success achieved in creating and managing the Business Intelligence assets.

Using the Key Performance Indicators

8-A

TBIA Business Intelligence
Capability Maturity Model'

Objectives

1. **Identify and Define What to Measure**
2. **Create Measurement Factors**
3. **Define a Measurement Scale**
4. **Define an Audit Metholodgy**
5. **Describe How to Use the Audit Results**

8-B

Key Performance Indicators

Management support
Business alignment
Business – IT partnership
Business goals-requirements
Integration
Scalability
Adaptability
Performance
Reliability
Ease of Use
Maturity
Scope & Comprehension
Velocity
Quality
Value

Key Performance Indicators have been identified and selected to be used in the audit and assessment of each of the components of the asset base. These Key Performance Indicators are also used in a separate over-all rating for the Business Intelligence Asset Base. Each Business Intelligence component has been divided into associated parts, which are identified in the Business Intelligence Capability Maturity Model as Key Assessment Features. These have been described in Chapter 3. These are also individual chapters for each Business Intelligence Component.

8-C

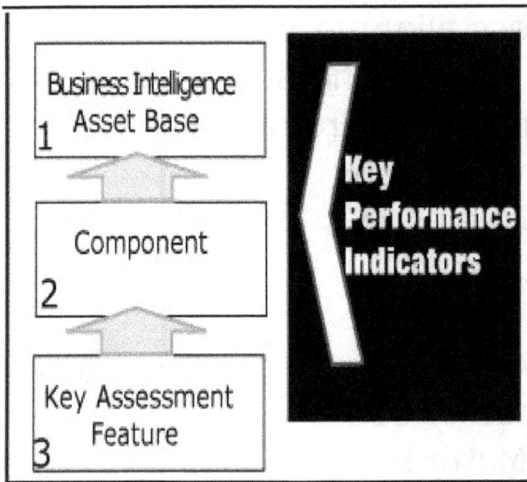

During the audit process, each of the Business Intelligence Asset Base - Key Assessment Features- will be reviewed and analyzed and a rating will be determined. The rating will be the result of an assessment of each feature using the applicable Key Performance Indicators. The component will also be rated based on the average and/or auditor's assessment of the total ratings for the Key Assessment Features.

The Business Intelligence Asset Base, as a whole, will be assessed using each of the Key Performance Indicators. Component ratings and the overall rating for the Business Intelligence Asset Base will be used to rate the organization and to determine the Level of Maturity which should be assigned to the organization.

Some Key Performance Indicators are relatively obvious during a review of Business Intelligence assets. These are usually easy to measure. Some Key Performance Indicators, however, may be transparent and not so easily recognized. Whether obvious or not so easy to find, it is critical to identify all the Key Performance Indicators which are relevant to the Business Intelligence Asset Base component being audited. The information included in the chapters for each Business Intelligence component should assist in these decisions.

The rating should include at least the following for each Key Performance Indicator and each part of the Business Intelligence Asset Base:

- some definition of the objectives for that Key Performance Indicator for that part of the Business Intelligence Asset Base, i.e. how should that Key Performance Indicator be reflected in the part of the Business Intelligence Asset Base under review, For example, scalability is reflected in the existing Hardware base as the capability to rapidly increase data access rates and performance as users and volumes increase.

2. Key Performance Indicators

2.1 Management Support

Management must, first of all, understand just what Business Intelli¬gence is and what it means to the organization. What are the products, the principles, risks, and realities? What are the benefits and costs? Then Management needs to make a conscious decision to accept the realities of today's business environment and to take the actions necessary to create, manage and use the organization Business Intel¬ligence assets effectively. This is a decision which must come from the highest levels of the organization management. Since Business Intelligence activities and assets cross all the internal boundaries and impact the whole of the organization, the results of any parochial, or local management, decision(s) will not be effective or successful. Integration of data, infrastructures and architectures demand that all the organization resources must act as a single unit.

Support Means. Developing a Business Intelligence Asset Base requires a lot of time, money and human resources. Sending out the word to 'do it' without the necessary allocation of resources is just not going to make it happen. Demanding a Return on Investment (ROI) for each individual project is, perhaps, a good rule of thumb, since it makes those involved carefully evaluate their plans and determine whether there is real value in the Business Intelligence application development project. However, expecting a tangible and definitive, documented Return on Investment for your total dollars spent on Business Intelligence is not a reasonable expectation. Resources spent on Business Intelligence must be evaluated in terms of both costs, as well as value returned. Those returns should be evaluated based, not just on short term, tangible factors, but on numerous other impacts to the organization, such as the medium¬to-long term value of better decisions made possible with the new Business Intelligence. Hard to measure! Managers who understand the value of Business Intelligence, spend the resources knowing that if the Business Intelligence projects are well planned and effective, the money is well spent.

Management support also means the willingness to accommodate changes to operations and internal management guidelines where necessary to leverage the Business Intelligence.

Management Support means spending resources for training, communications, and such initiatives as those for data quality, master data, and meta data - to ensure that the Business Intelligence products are of the highest quality.

Management support means auditing of the Business Intelligence Assets for the organization in order to provide for:
  · better understanding of Business Intelligence,
  · a baseline for continual management monitoring, and
  · a follow-up Action Response Program for improvement of Business Intelligence within the organization.

2.2 Business Goals and Requirements

Goals and Objectives. Management needs to define objectives for the organization. The goals are definitions of specific management plans and objectives which can be communicated to and used by the rest of the organization in running the business. These should include both strategic objectives and tactical goals. Strategic objectives are long term and these identify organization direction and planning strategies, i.e. up to five years or more. Tactical goals are short term, usually a year or less, and include goals which are designed to support the satisfaction of the long term strategic plans. For example, there may be short term goals which call for an addition of three new products for a specific product line or a 10% sales increase in identified products for the central regions.

Those organizations with the best Business Intelligence will gain the business advantage. The best Business Intelligence is dependent on what the organization needs. So management has a strong incentive to identify those business objectives and goals, What the current goals should be in the new global economy may be different than historically was the case. What should the goals for the organization be? In many cases an organization will review and find that the old goals which may have included volumes and revenues, might instead be centered around profit per sales unit. These kinds of management targets and business understandings must be communicated. They should become an integral part of the strategies and tactics for the Business Intelligence and Enterprise Data Warehouse communities. Setting the goals for the organization also sets the direction and contents for the Enterprise Data Warehouse and the corresponding Analytics Platform.

Requirements We define Business Requirements in a slightly different manner than Business Goals. The business requirements are at a lower level than business strategic objectives and tactical goals. They are directly tied to tactical business plans for the organization. These requirements should impact directly on the make up of individual subsets of the Business Intelligence Asset Base. The creators and users of the Business Intelligence data need to understand each of the business requirements. Each should be clearly written in actionable phrasing - e.g. provide those users who have direct communications with the customer all the information about that customer - as up to date as possible. Each new Business Intelligence application or enhancement should incorporate definite and specific business requirements and these requirements should match or be a subset of those necessary to meet the tactical plans for the organization.

2.3 Business Alignment

Business Intelligence plans and goals should reflect and match the business goals and plans for the organization. Business Intelligence is key to reaching the goals of the organization and achieving success. Those organizations with the best (in terms of organization requirements.) and most relevant Business Intelligence will gain a decided business advantage. The marketplace is global. Management should recognize the changes around them and change their business goals as necessary to meet the new challenges.

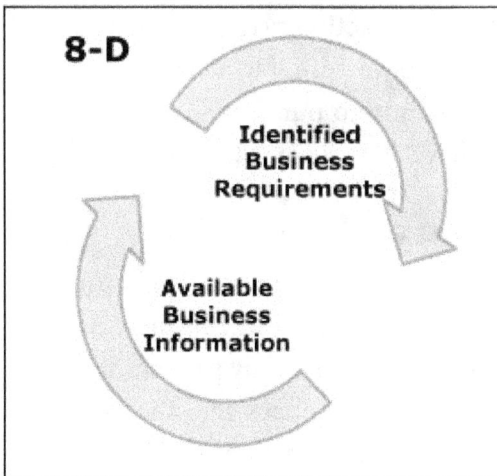

8-D

Identified Business Requirements

Available Business Information

Whatever the goals, however, they must be communicated to the organization and become an integral part of the strategies and tactics for the Business Intelligence community. Unless management has the right information at the right time to make the necessary decisions and shape the organization operations - individuals, management and the organization can and will flounder and fail. The 'right information' at the 'right time' are crucial descriptions. Tremendous amounts of resources may be expended, and usually are, for a comprehensive and workable Business Intelligence Asset Base. The returns from and the success of those expenditures is, in large part, dependent on how and where the resources are focused. What kinds of Business Intelligence are needed? When is it needed, i.e. how do we prioritize development? Management needs to identify, describe and com-municate business goals and associated Business Intelligence re-quirements to everyone in the organization.

Communication of the goals is not enough, however. The Business Intelligence applications and priorities must match and support the strategic and tactical goals of the organization. What does that mean? It means that there must be architectures and models which reflect the current state of the business. There must be an inventory of Business Intelligence applications and action prioritization based on business goals. Do this first because we need it to attain this goal, etc. Exactly what data do we need to add to our data warehouse to obtain this result? Do we already have what we need, or do we need to find out where it is and add it?

Management needs also to understand exactly what can and cannot be accomplished by creation and use of Business Intelligence. Also, the reverse is true. Business Intelligence may be only part of the answer. What else is needed? Response and feedback into the operations of the organization needs to be explored in parallel.

Translation of the Business Goals and Requirements demands skill and experience. Successful and strong definitions of these business goals and requirements will impact what Business Intelligence is available to the organization. Good and useful definitions are dependent on:

- management understanding of the Business Intelligence Asset Base
- management understanding of the organization and the place and goals of the organization within the business economy and marketplace.

Business Intelligence maturity and success is a product of the close integration of knowledgeable business users and Business Information which is the most comprehensive possible and which has been designed to give an excellent picture of the organization environment and realities.

Management Knowledge of the potential benefits and the specific products and uses for Business Intelligence is a prerequisite for realizing some of those benefits. By this, we mean that `if you don't know you can get it - you won't ask for it!'. And the correlation to this is: 'If the operational and information technology staff do not know what is needed, then they can not deliver it.' Guiding business and information technology resources in focusing on the Business Intelligence which most meets the organization needs requires management who know what can be delivered, then asks for it.

Identifying and developing the list of Business Information assets most needed to meet organization requirements requires a clear understanding and integration of the following:

- the business strategic and tactical requirements of the organization, and
- a clear understanding of exactly what Business Information it

is possible to deliver, given all the organization and industry capabilities, constraints, and available data.

Sphere of Influence. In most cases, Business Intelligence is aligned to the needs of the business. However, only a fraction of the benefits available from the Business Intelligence assets are realized if there is only a one way alignment. Business Intelligence can provide the push to translate traditional activities into information-based processes which flow more smoothly and allow leverage of the available information in ways not recognized before. Benefits may be much more dramatic if the business activities and resources can be aligned with Business Intelligence and changed to leverage the inherent potential within the Business Intelligence.

Any audit using this Key Performance Indicator, Business Alignment, should analyze the documentation and results for Business Intelligence to determine whether this dual alignment process has been considered and included in the plans for the project. Look also for results in the use of the Business Intelligence by the business community.

Sphere of Influence

8-C

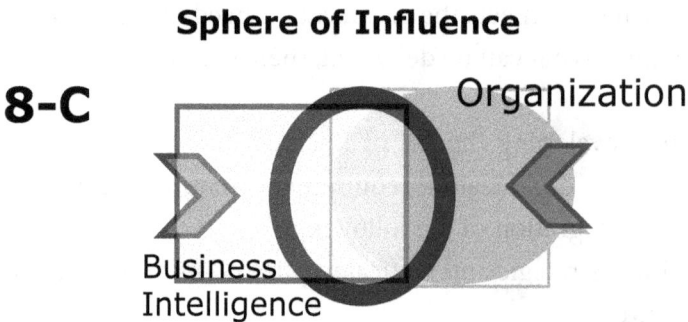

Organization

Business
Intelligence

2.4 Business & Information Technology Partnership

What does this mean? Knowledgeable business resources of the organization must work hand in hand with the information technolgy staff. With Business Intelligence, if one or the other group tries to 'go it alone', the consequences are often severe. Success always requires both. If the business people, as in the early stages of Business Intelligence maturity levels for an organization, try to develop their own business information - the results are most often a proliferation of desktop data bases and spread sheets. The results always seem to be acceptable to the small group which develops them, at least for the short period of time until they need more data from more data sources. When the Information Technology resources have built enterprise data warehouses - without the partnership with key business people -- the result most often is failure because 'no one comes to the party'.

What to look for in an audit Do the project plans have reasonable and detailed business goals and participation? Are (or does the documentation for the project show that) the planning and development meetings attended by both groups? Are Business users passionate about their Business Intelligence assets? Are the Information Technology staff happy with the usage of the Enterprise Data Warehouse? Is there good measurement documentation for usage? These are just some of the indicators at the organization level of the successful partnership of business and information technology resources in Business Intelligence.

An auditor needs to look for specific business/information technology collaboration as noted for each component of the model (see later chapters.)

2.5. Integration

Integration can be applied to data, to applications, to user interfaces, i.e. portals - just to name a few topics. For Business Intelligence,the primary integration of interest is for DATA. Data integration is a primary driver of all the structures and systems of a data warehouse, i.e. the Data Integration Platform. Data Integration is key to the creation of business information. As discussed in other chapters, data integration for Business Intelligence is achieved through two primary methods:

· federation - which is a virtual integration of several different data sources, usually managed by overlaying a map of the data over the physical data sources and treating them as a single entity. This kind of integration is fine for fast, low volume types of data processing. However, there are a number of issues with using it for any high volume data transactions. For example, performance of the source database is impacted. There is also an issue with the availability of historical' data, i.e. usually only the most current data is available.

· data warehouse - the platform and processes which collect data from multiple sources and unify it into a single library of information. The data is historical, i.e. collected at some point after the actual occurrence of the transaction activity. How long after depends on requirements and source data extraction methods. After the data is extracted and 'integrated' into a data warehouse platform, there should be no more issues with impacting the source system performance. And, of course, there is as much historical information as necessary to meet organization requirements. We can also process this data at will and spin it off into 'archival' data stores when data becomes too old and/or usage activity lessens.

Thus, the most basic construct of Business Intelligence is the collection of source data and the cleansing, transformation and integration into a data warehouse. This data integration is key to the availability of a single source of data which is uniformly formatted, has the same values and means the same thing, or is essentially, a `single source of truth' across the organization. These data from multiple, disparate application and operational data stores are brought together and turned into high quality, business information.

Audit Considerations - Business Intelligence Component level. The questions an auditor faces is how is the integration accomplished and how well is it accomplished. The auditor needs to look for specific integration factors during the audit, analysis and rating of the individual components of the Business Intelligence Capability Maturity Model. These integration factors are discussed and described in the chapters on each of the model components.

Audit Considerations - Organization level Business Intelligence. In assessing Business Intelligence at the organization level, we will combine the findings and ratings for integration within the model components - with an assessment for the organization Business Intelligence, as a whole. An overall assessment of the quality of integration for all Business Intelligence assets for the organization should include the review and analysis of several factors: What are the users saying about their Business Intelligence quality? How much trouble do the information technology specialists admit to in the alignment of the disparate data, including the need for replicated data sources and mechanisms other than standard integration processes through the Business Intelligence Engine driving software like Extract, Translate and Load. Auditors should look for documented evidence of problems.

Unless people across the organization see the same pictures of data and can access that data as a single 'truth' - then there is no way the organization can present a sustainable united business front. In early stages of Business Intelligence maturity of the organization, multiple silos of data are typical. Many sets of people, requirements, technology and data stores may exist. *Integration of the disparate data from across the organization is one of the strongest considerations which should be made in the rating of the Business Intelligence maturity of an organization.*

During any Business Intelligence audit, also look for any other areas where integration might be a factor. This may include infrastructures and architectures and any other component or key assessment feature which should include this Key Performance Indicator.

2.6 Scalability

Scalability

The capabiiilty to expand as necessary to accommodate more users, volumes of data, messages, transactions

Defined. Large scale Business Intelligence systems must support thousands of users who interactively access the same reports and data. Business Intelligence also must support massive amounts of data. Business Intelligence Scalability refers to the ability to meet the requirements of the organization in terms of number of users, type and number of reporting, applications, and data volumes. Scalability refers to the ability to support these increases in data, queries, users (i.e. all the load and access transactions) quickly, effectively, efficiently and with no downtime to the system.

Issues. Choosing vendors and products which will allow for both inherent scalability, as well as, where necessary, rapid and easy to accomplish upgrade, enlargements and enhancements is difficult. Integrating all into a set of architectures and an infrastructure which will not be broken by rapid increases in users and volumes of data is especially difficult. Sometimes a lot of money, time, sweat and tears can be expended in the process. How well a product scales often depends on what the requirements are within the organization. Some of the impacts can come from increases in the number of total users, number of reports, expansion of areas for data collection and integration, number of concurrent users. However, making the systems and infrastructures scalable, i.e. making it happen, is essential. To obtain the highest scalability, companies need a technology or set of technologies which reaches as many users as necessary. This is not a one time thing. Having a scalable system takes continuous monitoring, adjusting and reinvention on the part of the unsung information technology specialists - as well as the industry dreamers and suppliers of technology. In the later chapters on infrastructures and other components, some of the scalable features to look for are described in detail.

Scalability of the Business Intelligence platform is one of the most difficult assignments for Information Technology to manage. Consideration has to be given to internal requirements which may not be well understood at the time of vendor selection. How many internal users? What kind of response times? How complex are the queries? What percentage are simple canned report viewers vs interactive drill-down reports and ad hoc users who may have increasingly complex needs. Each of these requirements increases the need for scalability and some requirements are more difficult to satisfy than others. Since some vendors may have little real experience at deploying extremely large scale Business Intelligence platforms, sometimes it is a 'blind leading the blind' scenario in acquiring and integrating scalable Business Intelligence architectures.

In addition, of course, requirements may change dramatically as users begin to appreciate and want more Business Intelligence. Rising use and scalability issues can create performance nightmares and actually bring systems to a halt - if scalability has not been built into the platform and infrastructures.

Assessment. Building in scalability is hard. Assessing the lack of it in a Business Intelligence asset base is usually not difficult. Per formance issues will be apparent. Performance in terms of response times, especially at peak times of the day - i.e. highest volumes - is one key. Users will be happy to complain about query response times. More complex queries may be just impossible. The information technology support teams collect and keep reams of monitoring data. Any audit should include a review of the monitoring data, as well as, discussions with key power users and key information technology support staff. Look for more about scalability assessment in later chapters.

2.7 Performance

Defined. Performance in the Business Intelligence world refers to information access and presentation. Is the information presented to the user who wants it in a format which is easy to use and understand, at the 'right' time for the user to get the most value from the information.

Performance
Does the business information get to the 'right' user, at the 'right' time, and in the 'right' format for that user?

Background. The definition highlights only the tip of the iceberg results for Business Intelligence performance. Response times are crucial, and those response times must match the requirements of the users for the informa tion. When do we need the Business Intelligence? It can be one week after the fact; one day; several hours. Currently, the industry is pushing toward minutes, for very fast turnaround on operations reporting and management. Also, we expect to have Business Intelligence available online around the clock, to meet the needs in many cases for global operations. This means that there is a need for 24X7 operations.

Response time is the result of many factors - including
- analytic software
- business intelligence design
- data models
- database management system
- infrastructures
- data warehouse architecture
- portal/web interface
- complexity and form of query
- tools which load the data warehouse and the specific content

management stores.

These are only some of the factors which can influence performance.

When do we load the data from our multitude of data stores? Performance measures how well the combination of factors and components of the Business Intelligence base works and how well the results are presented to the end user. Can a user get the needed information in the right format and at the right time? The capabilities to meet these requirements make up the Performance factors. This is a very simple and straightforward definition. However, it is very difficult to make this happen.

One of the key things for analyzing performance is defining the requirements for measuring that performance. How fast is fast enough? Two days ,.. Two minutes .... Two seconds? What is the right format? Two words in response to a query; a full report of financial data.

Performance requirements must be integrated into the search for appropriate data base management systems - to logical data models and physical data stores which will speed up format and retrieval of data.

2.8 Product Quality

Product Quality

Is the Business Intelligence accurate, accepted as 'truth' across the organization, up to date and easy to understand and use.

Defined. The basic product is the data, i.e. the 'raw' product collected from multiple sources, e.g. the operational systems. The intermediate product is the business information which has been cleaned, translated and integrated. The final product is Business Intelligence, which is the business information which reflects the organization/business requirements in the collection, format and presentation, as well as, the marrying of that business information with the human end user (or intelligent automated system). The quality of that data is a result of the full range of treatment and driving factors within the Business Intelligence Asset Base.

Comments. The principal product of the Business Intelligence systems is Information --- i.e. data translated into information. This Quality Driver involves all the factors which ensure that the Data is accurate, formatted to meet the user needs, timely, and comprehensive enough to meet the business requirements. This also means that there is only a single version of the product. Any look at specific data should give the same answers. Data Quality is the subject of numer¬ous books, articles, program initiatives, and more. Some of these issues and suggested initiatives are discussed in later chapters.

Assessment. Audit and assessment of product quality is not quite as straightforward as might be thought. Because of the human factors involved, information which comes directly from Business Intel-ligence systems might be further edited by those who must use that information. This might mask poor quality data issues. Everything from spreadsheets to mental 'fudge' factors might be used by those who need correct data and know they are not getting it. However, in most cases, just asking the right questions and seeing the results of Service Level Agreements will give the auditor some idea of the quality of the data and trust placed by the business community in the information.

2.9 Ease of Use

It can be extremely difficult to describe exactly what is meant by 'user friendly' or 'ease of use'. In many cases, of course, it depends on who and what skills the user has. But, on the whole, we mean that any business user should be able to understand the language and constructs being used. We mean that a presentation should be graphical, well documented and guide a user through a series of 'windows' type screens. If the user is, or grows more, sophisticated, then the tools should evolve to meet that sophistication. We also mean that the business user should be able to understand the development tools and models and contribute to design and development. Right there, at the time of building a data model, is when the substance is built into a system - input by the user, at just that time, might make the difference in success or failure of the resultant Business Intelligence application. This means that data models and other development tools, like Computer Aided Systems Engineering tools, should be easily understood by anyone - including those who are not information technology specialists.

Review and assessment of tools and development processes, at minimum, should require that they be easy to understand and use. Ask the users who have tried them. Ask the Information Technology people who have tried to explain them.

2.10 Comprehension

Comprehension means just how complete is something. When referring to Data, do we have all that we need to meet the business requirements? Does a user have to follow another trail to find everything needed...e.g. anywhere else where you must look for completeness. In terms of meta data, do we have all the technical data that we need to follow a history of the data? Is the business meta data complete?

Review and assessment of all the components and overall Busi¬ness Intelligence Asset Base ALWAYS ask the question - Is it complete?

2.11 Value to Cost

How much did it cost in resources - time, money, human resources -- sometimes even 'blood, sweat, and tears'? How much value did and are we receiving from it? In most cases, in an audit, we are evaluating Business Intelligence systems, which may add new data or improve on what we have. In some cases, we may be auditing an upgrade to the infrastructures of the data warehouse or the purchase of a new analytic platform.

Sometimes it is very difficult to assess value. Most of the time it is not so difficult to determine costs. That frequently means that the tangible costs will outweigh the value, perceived value, and maybe even, the actual value. In any case, the auditor should identify whether there are efforts made to determine value to cost evaluations. Is there a documented method? Is there a mandatory review of estimated before and after the fact figures? How much reliance is and should be placed on the figures? How is value measured? All these should be evaluated and rolled into the overall evaluation for the Key Assessment Feature, the Business Intelligence Component, and the overall Business Intelligence Asset Base.

The Data Integration Platform

Chapter Contents

1. Enterprise Data Warehouse

1.1 Introduction

The Data Integration Platform supports the collection and integration of data from operational and other sources. The data is cleansed, reformatted, translated and integrated into a unified central library of information for the organization. This information is expected to be accurate, timely and easily accessible. It can be trusted by the organization for use in decision-making and to manage and improve organization performance. The Enterprise Data Warehouse is the industry recognized platform for data integration. It provides for all the data integration services and allows an organization to leverage its data resources and use them for making business decisions.

1.2 Primary Objectives.

The goals of an Enterprise Data Warehouse are to provide accurate, timely, consistent, reliable information for the organization. The information must be easily accessible and in a form which is flexible and easily adaptable to the needs of the users of the information, i.e. the data must be easily translated to satisfy the information needs of a wide variety of users. The users must be able to access any piece of the information and combine that slice of information with any other slice, in order to better understand and manage the business. The information must be secure. Access should be limited to those who have been granted the rights to view and use the data.

The goals for the Presentation Library of the Enterprise Data Warehouse include:

- Integrated data - i.e. Integration of data from multiple data sources;
- Data integrity and consistency. Cleaning, reformat and translation of data from disparate sources and frequently non¬aligned data elements into a single, organization-acceptable, uniform and commonly understood information library.
- Data Accuracy and Clarity. Quality of data is critical. This means that the data must be accurate and correct. There must be a clear understanding of what the data is and represents.

In other words, it must be translated into information of value. This requires, for one thing, that there is sufficient meta data associated with each piece of data, to supply all the information required to translate it and to provide clear tracking and audit information.

·   Time Based Data. The information about dates and times for each and every piece of data is of key importance.

·   Accessibility. Access needs to be easy, flexible, fast, and meet the requirements of the users. (The information structures must also meet the requirements of the Business Intelligence tools used by the organization.)

·   Data Security. Information Assets are protected, based on organization requirements, rules and standards.

1.3 Enterprise Data Warehouse Functions and Characteristics

Functions. The Enterprise Data Warehouse functions include: the extraction and collection of raw data;

·   the cleansing, translation and integration of that data;

·   the storage and management of the cleansed, reformatted and integrated information - for presentation and use for Business Intelligence applications.

The analytical tools and interfaces for Business Intelligence applications are described in a separate chapter on the Analytics Platform. The structure and data formatting within the presentation library may be impacted by the requirements of the analytical tools which

interface with the library - i.e. types and specific Business Intelligence toolsets.

Characteristics. The characteristics of an Enterprise Data Warehouse which were defined by Bill Inmon in the 1980's are that it is subject-oriented, non-volatile, time dependent and integrated. All of these characteristics are still, for the most part, accurate. However, there are some differences of opinion within the industry about what ` subject-oriented' means. These characteristics are further described below:

Subject Oriented. The subject orientation of a data warehouse is the property which indicates how the data is grouped. The subject orientation may be based on major data stubjects, i.e. products, customers, transactions. Another alternative is that the data is organized into groups based on business processes. This subject orientation is a major and deciding feature which differentiates the Kimball and the Inmon methods and architecture styles.

Non Volatile. The Enterprise Data Warehouse is an 'after-the-fact' information repository. Historical data is collected, integrated and stored. It does not change. It reflects what has already happened, i.e. history. The reality of just how long 'after the fact' is in a state of flux right now within the industry. As technologies get better and requirements evolve, Business Intelligence moves closer to the collection, integration and use of 'real time' or near real time transaction data. The term 'right time' has been coined to indicate that data should be a reflection of specific organization requirements. The collection and, integration and use of the real time or near real time data requires a completely different operational approach than the historical data collection. Essentially this is a new paradigm and the data is often stored separately or as a separate part of the Enterprise Data Warehouse.

Time Dependent. The data represents 'after the fact' or historical information. Date and Time are key to use and presentation. When was it collected, in what circumstances, when and how was it translated and integrated into the data warehouse. What does the data represent - time wise. A basic attribute, of course, relates to the time of collection and any other activities associated with the data. This information about data and time is necessary to the understanding of the data and must be associated with the data within the data warehouse library. The term, time, has been expanded here to include date and time.

Integrated. The many formats and copies of essentially the same data elements, which reside in various source data bases of multiple application systems, must be resolved into a single data point, within a structure of interrelated data - i.e. cleansed, translated, and integrated into a library of business information.

1.4 Audit Wheel for the Data Integration Platform.

With its long history and industry-accepted standards and practices, the Enterprise Data Warehouse is the foundation for the Data Integration Platform construct for the TBIA Business Intelligence Capability Maturity Model™.

This is the proven framework for leveraging the data of the organization into meaningful, business information - i.e. *the single source of truth.*

The audit wheel (figure 9-A) identifies all of the Key Assessment Features which should be reviewed during an audit. In this case, the subject is the Enterprise Data Warehouse. The Key Assessment Features (Figure 9-A) are used to divide and understand the concepts. In this chapter, each Key Assessment Feature of the Data Integration Platform is defined and described. (Note: The infrastructures of the Enterprise Data Warehouse are considered separate components and will be discussed in later chapters.) The focus is on understanding them well enough to assess and rate the component and Key Assessment Features during an audit of the Enterprise Data Warehouse.

9-A

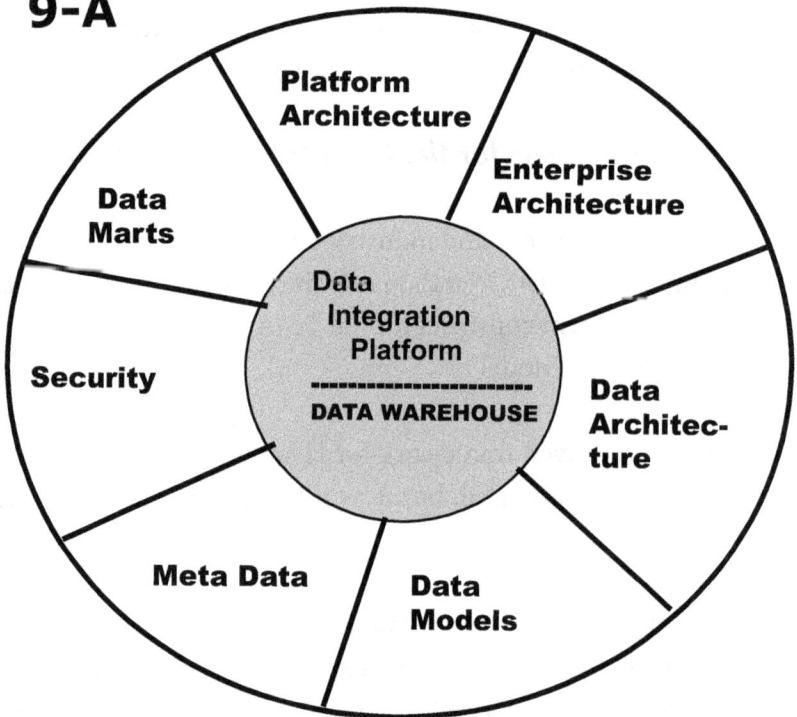

2. Key Assessment Features

2.1 Platform Architecture

2.1.1 The architecture of the Enterprise Data Warehouse includes the following:

Source Systems.   Operational systems which capture the transactions / activities of the organization. These source systems are not considered within the scope of the TBIA Business Intelligence Capability Maturity Model™, i.e. part of the Enterprise Data Warehouse. They are included in the discussion only because most of the data which is brought into the Enterprise Data Warehouse comes from these source systems.

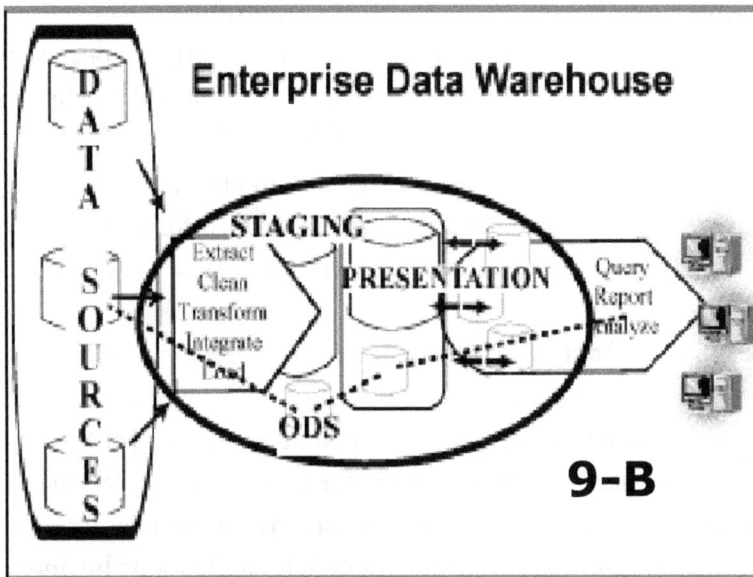

Data Staging Area. This is a storage and work in process area for the data which comes into the data warehouse. This area includes all the data files, databases, tools, and processes which clean, trans¬form, integrate, archive (support, replication and management of aging data) and for the other support & maintenance activities, plus any other intermediate processing requirements. This area may be considered logically as a single unit. However, in reality, there may be numerous flat files, databases, servers, and working spaces. This is considered the back room area of the Enterprise Data Warehouse. No Query of the data should be allowed. This is a working environment. Among many other things, this is where data is cleaned, reformatted, and integrated into the overall architecture and structures to meet the requirements of the Enterprise Data Warehouse presentation library.

Presentation Library Area. This is the environment which hous¬es the information which is used for direct querying, report writers, and other business intelligence analytical applications (i.e. interfaces to the Analytical Platform). This may be explicitly termed the Data Warehouse in much of the industry documentation, which actually makes a lot of sense, i.e. the 'warehouse' of information which is available in structure, content and format available to end users.

Operational Data Store. There is some confusion and blurring of the definition and use for this area. One definition indicates that this ODS area is real time, or very current, data, with less of an em¬phasis on history than the Presentation Library. This Operational Data Store may be a datastore which is used as an interim area for the Data Warehouse. This interim area may be updated by business operations. It is designed to quickly perform simple queries on small amounts of data. (e.g. answering a customer query.) Very recent data is stored here. (Operational Data Systems were originally developed as an administrative reporting system, usually updated daily.)

Data Mart. A data mart may be either the primary data store used in the data warehouse for both elementatry data and for summarized and aggregated data, as in the Kimball architecture. Or the Data Mart may be simply a logical subset of the data warehouse presentation library. In either case, a data mart may include summarized and/or aggregated data. Usually the data mart objectives are focused on meeting the specialized needs of a particular group of users.

2.1.2 Two Building Methods. There are two primary philosophies and architecture styles for designing and creating an Enterprise Data Warehouse. A few of the major differences in the two approaches are the differing data models; the Data Integration Architecture and the Development Approach.

	KIMBALL	INMON
Data Models	Dimensional	EDW -Normalized Data Marts - Dimensional
Data Integration Architecture	Conformed Data Data Warehouse Bus	Normalized Data Structures
Deveelopment Methodology	Business Process Iterative Integrated Data Marts	Centralized Structures Iterative

Inmon method: Central libraries, designed using normalized data models, which contain the data at an elementary detail level. Associated data marts which are dimensional and which have summarized and/or aggregated level data. The data marts are not considered as part of the Enterprise Data Warehouse. Integration relies on the nature of the normalized data structures.

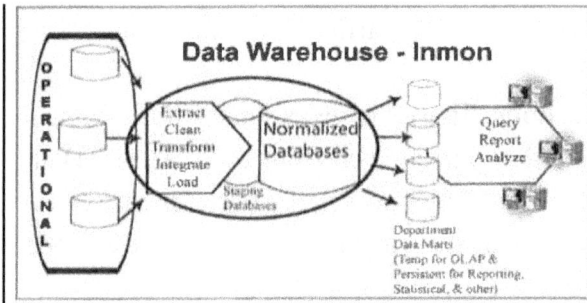

9-C

Kimball method: Central library, designed using dimensional data models, which contain the data at the elementary detail level. Associated data marts which are dimensional and which have summarized and/or aggregated level data. All are considered to be part of the Enterprise Data Warehouse. Integration uses conformed data tables. (note - conformed means that exactly the same definitions and formats are mandated.)

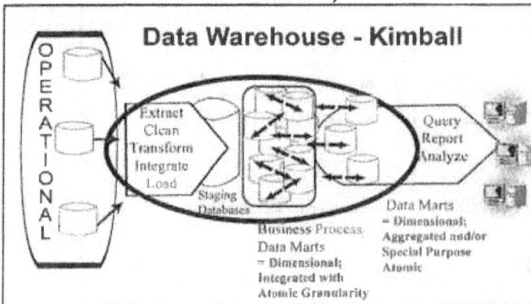

9-D

2.2 Enterprise Architecture

Enterprise Architecture is defined and used here in two different ways

1. Enterprise Architecture refers to the physical structures and con-structs of the organization.

2. Enterprise Architecture can also refer to a set of models, constructs and documents which management has developed as a blueprint to guide the organization.

2.2.1 Physical Architecture

Service Oriented Architecture (SOA). The Enterprise Data Warehouse can no longer exist in isolation. There are some major changes which are occurring in the industry which impact the interface and relationships of the Enterprise Data Warehouse with the rest of the organization. In many cases, Service Oriented Architectures (SOA) have become integral to the foundation infrastructures of an organization.

SOA is an architectural style which allows for easy interoperability and communications among applications, whatever the platform. SOA divides, i.e. segments, applications and components into simpler, functionally complete pieces. An application, which was formerly a single program may be comprised of many generic parts or services, which may be, in turn, used by multiple applications. (i.e. 'off the shelf programming and interoperability constructs) Ar-chitectural services, which provide for transmission of data among various platforms and applications may be comprised of multiple smaller functionally complete pieces. Each of the functional pieces are distinct and independent. They are called services. These services may be grouped together, depending on the needed functionality, to perform tasks. The independence of the functional pieces allow for sharing of the business or technical 'services for multiple applications. The organization can build and use only those func-tional pieces which provide the necessary services specific to the organization requirements.

Where enterprise architectures have changed, the interfaces of the Enterprise Data Warehouse must reflect the changes. Instead of a standard, platform to platform, extraction of data from application data stores, the collection and distribution process may be changed to include such features as 'web services'.

Streaming data. The organization may have moved to 'real time' or near real time data collection. This most likely will mean that the organization is using 'streaming data' from the operational data sources rather than regularly scheduled data extractions. Since this is an entirely new paradigm for the industry, auditing this process will require a comprehensive research of the organization practices.

2.2.2 Architecture Blueprints

There are at least three different parts of an Enterprise Architecture blueprint which will impact the Enterprise Data Warehouse.

A.   **Strategic Objectives and Tactical Goals**

B.   **Master Data Management Map**

C.   **Applications Inventory and Planning Guide**

If an Enterprise Architecture is available and includes these features, then the organization is clearly a leader in this area. The fact that these topics are documented is evidence that management has spent some time on conceptualizing and planning. There must be an understanding about the requirements for Business Intelligence and other Information Technology needs. Although the rest of the Enterprise Architecture may be of interest for Business Intelligence needs, the following three topics are crucial.

A.   Strategic Objectives and Tactical Goals

The most ideal documentation would include clearly stated and defined Objectives and Goals. There should also be an inventory of applications, both for transactional and business intelligence. This inventory should reflect a direct association with a list of Business Intelligence requirements. The planned data additions for the Enterprise Data Warehouse should be relatively easy to decipher from such a set of goals and requirements. This would also mean that there is some clear evidence of management support and Business Alignment with Business Intelligence Goals - two of the Key Performance Indicators which are to be rated during the audit process.

B.   Master Data Management Map

There may be program initiatives underway within an organization to provide clear identification, descriptions and integration of refer ence data or subject data which is uniform and easily adapted across the organization. Anyone or any application which has need of the data would be constrained by the definitions, formats and other information about data which is included in the formal Enterprise Architecture. (The Conformed tables which provide the integration for the Kimball methodology essentially fulfill a large part of these requirements.) This could make a very real difference in the creation of an integrated set of data and make the whole process of creation and integration much easier.

C. Applications Inventory and Planning Guide
This is the Inventory discussed in Section A. The existence of an Applications Inventory would indicate an excellent support base by management. There is a lot of work and planning which is involved in developing such an inventory. Much of the work includes the identification of business objectives and goals and the creation of targets which will allow the Business Intelligence area to meet the requirements of the business.

2.3 Data Architecture
2.4 Data Models

How the data is designed and structured is important to the accessibility and usability of the Enterprise Data Warehouse. Two of the major characteristics to be considered are:

    a. the design of the data base storage structures, and

b. the methods used to integrate the data.

The physical data stores are designed and structured using *Logical Data Models,* which are maps detailing the layout and potential access paths of data within the physical data structures.

The two principal design possibilities for the data base models and resulting storage structures are normalized and dimensional.

Normalized Data Models.

A normalized data model is a logical database design which separates data into discrete, unique entities, i.e. relational tables, The structure of the data in the normalized data model closely resembles the data as used in the business and is based on subject data, i.e. products, customers, etc.. With this structure, there can be only one table for each data object. Each of these data objects, i.e. relational database tables, are connected to all the other data objects through known associations within the data. This very simple sounding concept has several complex and unique results.

1 First, it is a very difficult and cumbersome task to create a normalized data model. The process demands that information technology specialists do the work. The result is that business people are frequently not closely involved with the process.

2.   This normalized data model removes data redundancy by

the separation of the data into the discrete entities.

3.   Normalization of the data also provides the basis for integration of the data. The data is present only once in the model and all the data relationships are built directly into the physical structure of the data.

The Normalized Data Model is basic to the data architecture used by the Inmon Enterprise Data Warehouse.

Dimensional Data Models.

A dimensional data model is a logical database design which optimizes the data structure to make it easy to use in access and use of the data for management decision support, i.e. easy to access, fast responsive query performance. The data is architected in the form of a star schema. The fact tables contain the measurements and the dimension tables hold the information which describes exactly what is known about those measurements, e.g. products and times related to the measurement of the transaction in question, say the sale of a grocery item. The structure is called a star schema because of the single measurement table which is associated with many surrounding dimension tables.

The Kimball approach to the construction and integration of data within the Enterprise Data Warehouse mandates that all the data be designed and stored using Dimensional Models. There are data dimensional tables built for data at an elementary level of granularity. There are also separate dimensional tables created for data at summarized and aggregated levels, also called data marts. These are closely tied to the related detailed tables and are considered as part of the Enterprise Data Warehouse.

More about Logical Data Models

Logical Data Models are the front end to the physical data stores. They are the easy to understand and use pictures which can be automatically translated by the software into the physical data stores. One of the most important aspects of the use of these models is operational. How are the logical data models created and used. And, subsequently, when a change is made, is the change made to the logical data model and fed through to the physical data model and data. The audit process should include some analysis and review of the operational and physical aspects of the logical data models and physical data stores.

Audit Guidelines.

There are several considerations to be made in audit of these Key Asset Features. The auditor should check on how the organization is designing and structuring the data and, in parallel, what are the data models which are being used. This usually just means asking several people who do the job. They should be able to guide you through the process and provide some documentation and data results.

' Either of the two primary archtectures for the Enterprise Data Warehouse, i.e. Inmon or the Kimball approach, have been proven to be successful. However, the auditor needs to ensure that the following questions are considered and answered:

1.   Is there a clear understanding and application of the selected method. The auditor should ensure that those who design and manage the Business Intelligence assets have a clear under-standing of the selected approach. Look for data modeling speciality groups for the normalized data bases. Check with those who are designing. Find out exactly what are their goals for the data stores. Do they understand how the data is being integrated?

2.   Is the selected method used uniformly. Make sure that there is no ambiguity about the application and use of the design and construction methods and processes. For example, if all the data structures are dimensional, then there must be an integrating BUS structure, i.e. conforming data. Find out how the architecture is defined and applied. There may be disagreement within the organization among the designers and managers of the process about which approach, Kimball or Inmon methodology, should be used. This is important. If some Business Intelligence applications are designed using one and some another, then the results can be chaotic, at best. Integration of the data can suffer if there is no uniform application of the selected architecture.

2.5 Meta Data

Meta Data is described in a separate chapter, as a separate com-ponent of the Business Intelligence Asset Base. However, there should be some review of meta data in the context of the Enterprise Data Warehouse. The auditor needs to review the meta data within the Enterprise Data Warehouse. This review should include comprehension, formats, and accessibility. The three types of meta data are:

a.   technical meta data which is created and follows the movement of data across the Enterprise Data Warehouse;

b.   administrative meta data, which provides all the audit information about the data, e.g. who created, data created, date archived, etc.

c.   business meta data, which provides all the associated business definitions and other necessary business information about the data.

The auditor should check the following: Is the meta data created, and is everything captured which is needed. This includes ensuring that information statistics are captured for any movement within the Enterprise Data Warehouse.

2.6. Security

The Enterprise Data Warehouse contains a comprehensive information library for the organization.. This means there can be some very sensitive data included. The data security requirements will range from freely available to all to highly confidential. In fact, the information library could contain governmentally regulated data, like customer health records, which are protected by law, or proprietary product information which are subject to industrial espionage. The highly confidential information may be isolated into entirely separate data bases which are accessible only to those with the proper credentials. However, these data may also be included in the common information library and protected using views or stored procedures for access restriction. The organization may also have decided to encrypt the most highly sensitive information. In most cases, the data is accessible through the standard 'role based' identifications and passwords of the remainder of the organization information technology system.

For the audit, become familiar with the security needs and protec¬tion methods employed within the organization. To do this, find the right specialists and also do some more in depth research on up to date security methods and organization rules and systems. This field changes rapidly. This means if the organization has some particular security needs, make sure the audit team has the background and the knowledge of current industry standards and practices.

2.7 Data Marts

Data Marts are considered as a separate Key Assessment Feature for several reasons. For a mature Enterprise Data Warehouse, the data within the data marts are integral parts of the whole library and are integrated into the enterprise library. However, for initial Business Intelligence environments, this might not be true. The data marts may be silos of data. Any audit team needs to research and review the existing data marts and determine how the data is integrated into an organization library of information. If there is no integration then rate the organization no higher than a level 1 on this Key Assessment Feature, as well as the overall rating for the Organization.

3. Auditing

The rating chart in Figure 9-E may be used in the assessment of the Enterprise Data Warehouse. (See Chapters 3, 4, and 5 for more details on using the Capability Maturity Model constructs for auditing.)

Each of these Key Assessment Features for the Enterprise Data Warehouse is described in this chapter. When reviewing the type of architectures, data models, and other Key Assessment Features, note and rate the warehouse on the audit research and results obtained, not on any bias towards one or another of the principal architectures. Be sure, however, to clarify the results related to how the particular design method in use meets the requirements of each Key Performance Indicator. These Key Performance Indicators are described and audit details are provided in Chapter 8.

All ratings should be on a scale of 1 to 5, with 5 as the highest rating, i.e. the organization shows the highest level of maturity based on their requirements, industry technology and the impressions of the auditor. Use the information in Chapters 3, 4, and 5, and chapter 6, on the Levels of Maturity for the Business Intelligence Capability Maturity Model.

Rate each Key Assessment Feature for each of the KPI's. Rating should be 1 to 5, with 5 as hightest rating. See the appropriate chapter for audit and rating guidelines	Management	Support	BUSINESS	ALIGNMENT	PARTNER	SHIP	Business	Goals	Scalability	INTEGRATION	ADAPT	ABILITY	PERFORMANCE	USER	FRIENDLY	COMPREHENSION	HENS	QUALITY	VALUE
KEY PERFORMANCE INDICATORS																			
Platform Architecture																			
Enterprise Architecture																			
Data Architecture																			
Data Models																			
Meta Data																			
Security																			
Data Marts																			
Enterprise Data Warehouse																			

Give an overall rating to the Enterprise Data Warehouse based on the following:

· Assess and rate each of the Key Assessment Features. Give the Enterprise Data Warehouse - overall - a rating using a summation/average of these individual ratings.

· Assess and rate the Enterprise Data Warehouse - overall - using each of the Key Performance Indicators.

Levels of Competency:

· Level 1 - if there are independent data marts, with no established integrating architecture, rate the organization no higher than a Level 1.

• Rate the organization Business Intelligence as Level 5 only if the following are in place and operating successfully:

1. Both structured and unstructured data - integrat-ed

2. User self service - for the Presentation Library and meta data,

3. A comprehensive web based Enterprise Meta Data Library.

4. Search features similar to best of the online ca-pabilities.

5. Operational Business Intelligence - 'streaming data' for real time or near real time functions.

If 1 through 4 are in place and successful, the auditor may assign a rating of 5. There should be some consideration here regarding the requirements of the organization for the real time data. Assign the '5' rating, if there are no obvious requirements for real time.

10

The Analytics Platform

Chapter Contents

1. Introduction

2. Key Assessment Features

3. Audit Guidelines

1. Introduction

The Business Intelligence Analytics Platform supports all user interface for the business information in the data warehouse library. All of the query, analysis, reporting and online analytical processing which make up business intelligence applications for an organization are included in this arena of the Business Intelligence Asset Base. The focus of this chapter is on the architecture, categories of decision support and analysis, and other aspects of the *analytic platform.*

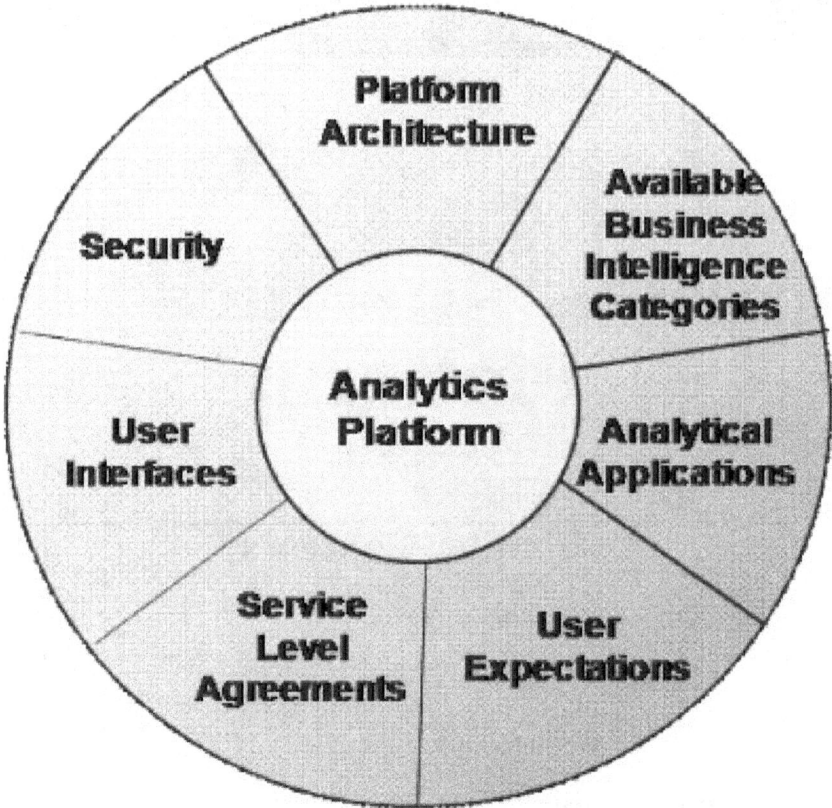

10-A   Key Assessment Features - Analytics Platform

The Key Assessment Features of the Analytics Platform are iden
tified in Figure 10-A. Each of these Key Assessment Features is described in this chapter. The final section will discuss Audit Guidelines for the Analytics Platform.

2. Key Assessment Features

2.1. Platform Architecture

The Analytical Platform includes the following:

A. Presentation Services - This includes:

·   the direct interface with the user, i.e. how the user sees and interacts with the information. The interface should be easy to use and intuitive for the business user. This most often means a graphical user interface (GUI) and common business terminology. Both should be simple and intuitive. The underlying layers of the Architecture should be transparent to the user. For example, users should not be required to know or use SQL statements and there should be no hunting for data.

·   delivery mechanisms. The user may access a special web portal for all standard reporting needs or the reports may be delivered via email. Also, users may have access to specialty Business Intelligence software which allow for direct query and analysis by the user.

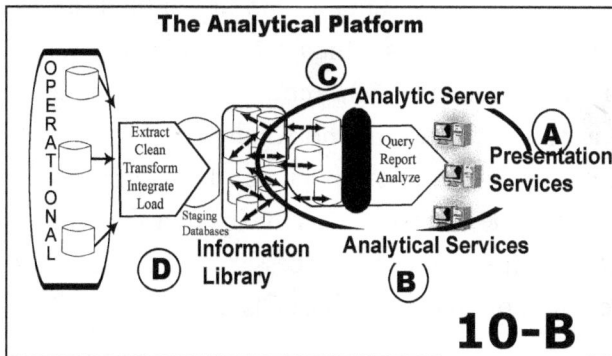

B. **Analytical Services.** This includes the underlying func-tionality behind the presentation services. There should be a wide range of analytical services available to an end user, based, of course, on the requirements associated with the business processes under review.

The user may access the Business Intelligence analysis func-tions through ad hoc data access using one of the organization supported Business Intelligence toolsets, e.g. like Cognos, Hyperion, or Business Objects. There may be sandard reports.

C. **Analytical Server.** This is where the end-user requests are processed (i.e. obtaining the reports and data). This server is also where security, administration, monitoring and other support activities take place. (See further notes on the servers in the later chapter on The Technical Infrastructure.)

D. **Information Library.** The Information Library which is accessed may be any one of several data stores. There are stand-alone data marts, the presentation library of the Enterprise Data Warehouse or data marts which are associated with or part of the data warehouse. The data models and databases which are directly accessed for use in the Analytical Platform should be structured to provide for simplicity and performance in getting the data out of the database. This means that the library must be in a form which provides the necessary dimensional structures. (see discussion on data models in Chapter 9)

2.2 Styles and Categories of Business Intelligence.

The organization needs to be able to deliver at least the following functions and styles of Business Intelligence:

A.   Query

Anyone should be able to access the data warehouse pre-sen-tation library using standard SQL or query tools. These queries can access any data within the data base and the questions may be in any format which is acceptable SQL, i.e. in a format which can be understood by the data base.

B.   Standardized Reports

The standard, persistent reports are created and made avail¬ble to satisfy specific business requirements. These are Business Intelligence reports which are produced and delivered on a regular basis to those users who need them. These reports should not be confused with the old versions of two dimensional printed reports. These are three dimensional and the user can drill down for information at more detailed levels. There is also drill across functionality which, in effect, will provide a broader view (i.e. more data). The report package is complete with all the relevant data, report for mats, and the mechanisms for analysis. The data necessary for the report is extracted from the data warehouse and is included with the report. The report package may be presented via a portal or sent via e-mail. Since this is a report package, the report could include sales for a product line for all regions by week, month and year. The report might be published each week with the latest data. Each user could see the overall USA sales by product for the week, for the month to date, and for the year (or whatever time frames might be required.) With the drill down features, the user could then see any or all products for any region or sales territory. With the drill across features, the user might add and view two or more separate sales territories.

The reports may be formatted as spread sheets, i.e. matrix, layouts or they may be custom, specially formatted reports. In most cases, there is a built-in refresh feature which will allow the update of the report by extracting the latest data from the data warehouse and reformatting the 'report'.

C.   Ad-Hoc Analysis

Ad hoc refers to the direct access of the primary data warehouse presentation libraries (including data marts) for Business Intelligence analysis.

D.   Online Analytical Processing (OLAP)

This term was derived from the previous OLTP, i.e. online transaction processing. This approach can provide quick answers for queries which require a multidimensional answer. In fact, speed of response is a primary factor in deciding to use this type of analysis. The data model is multidimenional, similar, in fact, to the dimensional models already described. The query output is usually displayed as a matrix, with the dimensions displayed as the rows and columns. The data values are the measures. This includes a presentation which is similar to the standardized reports in B.

The data for the OLAP query and analysis is built in the form of a cube. This cube of data has essentially the same characteristics and content structure as the dimensional data model of a data mart, i.e. includes dimensions, measures, and a star structure to hold the data values.

MOLAP - Multidimensional Online Analytical Processing. This is essentially the cube technology of certain vendors like Cognos. MOLAP allows high speed analysis of data through the use of a multidimensional data model, MO-LAP uses pre-computation and storage of information in the cube, i.e. snapshot data from the main data warehouse presentation library. Probably the most crucial factor in providing the speed of analysis is that these cubes are of aggregated and summarized data, i.e. the granularity is changed and in some cases, the dimensions may be grouped.

ROLAP - Relational On Line Analytical Processing - Both ROLAP and MOLAP analytic tools are designed to allow analysis of data through the use of a multidimensional data model, ROLAP does not use a pre-computation and storage of information. Instead, RO-LAP tools directly access the primary, relational data warehouse library.

E. Dashboards and Scorecards
These are charts and other graphics which report a short hand, 'picture' version of what is happening across the organization - based on predefined requirements. Dashboards report what is happening. Scorecards are usually ifferent in that the reporting is compared to some predefined measures and filters to

identify how well the organization is doing in the specific areas being reported. These scorecards may be part of a 'balanced scorecard' approach to monitoring and managing business.

F.   Forecasting and statistical analysis

These are usually complex and specialized Business Intelligence applications and data stores. The results require in depth search and analysis of the specialized data bases. At some level, most of the search, analysis and filter of the data will be by specialty software and/or specialists. The goal is to extract useful information from large sets of data which has been collected and integrated into a single library. The users of these types of applications are also, most often, trained specialists. The specialty data bases may have entirely different formats and may even be in separate libraries.

G.   Event or threshold triggers and alerts

These are predefined events or data values which are defined and set up to act like alarm clocks to set off some notification or event. These may be checks for tolerance or event levels and trigger events like special reports, scorecards, events or special e-mail notifications. Creation and distribution of Dashboards or Scorecards may be triggered in this manner. However, the usual practice is for Dashboards and Scorecards to be distributed on a regular basis. There may even be special triggers which will make updates or changes to the data in the library.

H. Analytical Applications

These are guided analytics, which are rule based, predesigned and developed set of processes, tasks, screens and data analysis. This is a function based application where the required user tasks and objectives have been carefully studied and incorporated. The standard operating practices and procedures involved in managing some part of the business have been defined and incorporated into a computer based, guided application. See the following section for a more complete definition.

2.3 Analytical Applications

There is a lot of potential in the industry and individual organizations for customized Business Intelligence applications. These custom¬ized applications could be used to guide users in the performance of a set of business tasks or processes to satisfy business requirements. Essentially the rules, the user guided processing and directions, and the relevant data can be integrated into an analytical application.

Business Intelligence applications include, among other things, a set of data or business information and the Analytical Application which allows the user to interface with that information. The interface may be with OLAP or other vendor toolsets (or internally created applications). We will borrow the definition for the Analytical Application from a report by Wayne W. Eckerson, (Development Techniques for Creating Analytic Applications; The Data Warehousing Institute, March, 2005)

An analytical application consists of a series of logically integrated, interactive reports, including dashboards and scorecards, that enable a wide range of users to access, analyze, and act on integrated information in the context of the business processes and

tasks that they manage in a given domain, such as sales, service,
...

Thus, the Analytical Application has four key ingredients (again from Eckerson. The Analytical application is:

1. Logically Integrated - includes business logic which helps a user move toward a decision and action - i.e. a guide through interactive reports and/or views of data.

2. Interactive reports that enable users to access, analyze, and act - Users can move up or down through various levels of data and reporting or add more information for greater clarity and analysis possibilities.

3. Integrated Information - The basic information being accessed is subject or business process oriented and the data is focused on the specific needs of the user. If the Data Integration Platform has been well architected - the remainder of the Enterprise Information Base is also readily available.

4. The Functionality of the Analytical Application addresses and meets the requirements for a specific Business do-main - e.g. sales, service, or manufacturing.

Eckerson believes, and we agree, that the term 'Analytical Application' has become vague, due to the industry focus on tools and technologies versus the Business Intelligence output. A central theme of this definition is that the Analytical Application is not just a set of reports, but is a guided map to analysis of the information. One of the evolutions occurring in the field is the incorporation of some of this 'guided analysis' approach into tools like dashboards and scorecards. These are becoming richer in context and capabilities.

Unfortunately, this class of Business Intelligence analysis is not yet well developed. The practice needs to be encouraged. There are several key advantages to building these types of Business Intelligence systems. These analytical applications:

- can capture and preserve the knowledge base and practices of those specialists in the organization who hold the key in their business arenas for keeping the business running effectively.
- provide the tools necessary to incorporate the business model and rules for business functions which are very complex and allow these functions to be handled by relative newcomers.
- provide consistency and accuracy for the functions included in the application.
- are inherently faster to an answer or function objective.

2.4 End User

Who are the Users? There are several different types of users and they can be grouped by how they interface with the analytical applications and interfaces. First is the end user who needs and uses the predesigned and developed analytical reports. This user rarely does more than report viewing and simple drill down or across activities. Another category of user is the power user who is most often a business analyst or specialist who analyzes the information in greater depth and on a regular basis. This power user frequently may also create new reports and make them available to the other users in the system. The developers of the reports and the analytical applications are most often Information Technology staff, in combination with these business specialists.

2.5 End User Expectations

The primary objective of the Analytical Platform is to deliver information for decision support to the 'client' - i.e. end users, directly or through specialized tools. These clients require fast, easily accessible, quality information. A great deal, i.e. most of the information, will be delivered in predefined formats and packaged for easy analysis. The analysis for these clients, in most cases, will be in the form of drilling down or across the information, based on focused measures and dimensions.

The end user expectations make several features mandatory for interface and reporting. It should be
- Easy to use -- i.e. easy and intuitive for the business user
- Web based, i.e. universal access
- Enterprise supported toolsets, which provide useful built-in functionality and are simple, flexible and easy to use, i.e. OLAP based
- High performance access (response based on user requirements) - requiring, among other things, data which is stored in a dimensional format which is designed and optimized specifically for user interface performance

In the near future, we should also see the incorporation of several additional features:
- both structured and unstructured data,
- good search engines which should match the capabilities of the best of the web engines
- easy, universal quick access and design which does not require any special training.

Although, this would necessarily be transparent to the users, there should also be automated update of the volumes of reports in the organization decision support library. Actually, something many organizations do not have today is an inventory of those analytical documents, reports and applications. Also, to be truly effective, a comprehensive Enterprise Meta Data Repository should also be online.

2.6 Service Level Agreements

Service Level Agreements are key to providing consistent and quality Business Intelligence to business users. These are contracts between those who are responsible for creating and delivering Business Intelligence, usually the Information Technology groups, and the end users. These Service Level Agreements incorporate such topics as levels of performance which will be delivered - i.e. timing, formats, and quality and comprehension of data.

2.7 Security

Security issues for the Analytical Platform are primarily handled within the infrastructures and data stores. The delivery mechanisms and user access to secure data within the libraries should be audited to ensure that there are no lapses. This should require some random validation of security passwords and report access procedures.

3. Audit Guidelines

In assessing the Presentation Services and the Analytical Services areas of the Analytical Platform, the auditor should review such questions as: How long does it take to learn the application or tool?

How fast is the work done? Do the users like using the application or tool? How complete is the application, in terms of required functionality and extension to tools like spreadsheets? For toolsets, e.g. OLAP, there should be a full range of services, like simple and complex queries and full analytical capabilities, including What? and Why? which are presented in easy to understand formats.

User Expectations should be assessed in terms of nature and level of demand for services. There should be Service Level Agreements for every set of Business Intelligence reporting and data. Business Intelligence applications are usually created for small groups of users at a time. The auditor should be able to identify these groups, identify what the goals for the Business Intelligence Application were and determine how well those goals were met. This is in addition to auditing the overall effectiveness and satisfaction with the analytical services.

There are several topics to be addressed:
   · How well do the platform, the software, and the services work technically? Are the performance statistics col¬lected and documented? Are the Business Intelligence toolsets working as planned and what are the issues or problems with them?
   · What are the expectations of the various categories of users? Have these expectations been managed and are they realistic? Interview users from all the categories of users, including the power users. Are the Service Level Agreements for performance being created, addressed and consistently met.
   • What is the satisfaction level of the users?
There are many things which can be measured within the technical aspects of the Business Intelligence Asset Base. One of the most crucial aspects, however, is how well the Business Intelligence being used to manage the business and to make things easier for the business resources. Ask them. And listen to the answers.

Audit Rating

Each of the Key Assessment Features has been described in this chapter. Review each of these features as they relate to and are employed by the organization. Assess each for the relevant Key Performance Indicators. These Key Performance Indicators are described and audit details are provided in Chapter 8.

All ratings should be on a scale of 1 to 5, with 5 as the highest rating, i.e. the organization shows the highest level of maturity based on their requirements, industry technology best practices and the impressions of the auditor. Details for rating the Key Assessment Features as a 0, 1, or 5 are included in this section. However, for those ratings of 2, 3, and 4, the auditor should follow the general guidelines given in Chapters 3. 4, and 5, as well as in Chapter 6, Levels of Maturity, for the TBIA Business Intelligence Capability Maturity Model™

Levels of Competency:
- Level 1 - Rate the Analytical Platform as 0 or 1, if there is not an Enterprise Data Warehouse or other integrating constructs.
- Level 5 - Rate the Analytical Platform as 5 only if there are some special leadership topics which have been ad-dressed and incorporated. This might include such things as Analytical Applications; integration of unstructured data; comprehensive meta data including an Enterprise Meta Data Repository; web based, general user access, with a global search engine; and generally high ratings on all Key Assessment Features.

Rate each Key Assessment Feature for each of the KPI's. Rating should be 1 to 5, with 5 as highest rating. See the appropriate chapter for audit and rating guidelines.	MANAGEMENT	SUPPORT	BUSINESS ALIGNMENT	PARTNERSHIP	BUSINESS	GOALS	SCALABILITY	it y	INTEGRATION	ADAPT	ABILITY	PERFORMANCE	ACCURE M	USER FRIENDLY	COMPREHENSION	QUALITY	VALUE
Platform Architecture																	
Analytical Categories																	
Analytical Applications																	
User Expectations																	
Service Level Agreements																	
User Interface																	
Security																	
The Analytics Platform																	

KEY PERFORMANCE INDICATORS

Key Assessment Features

Business Intelligence Engine

Chapter Contents

1. Introduction

This Business Intelligence Engine is the powerhouse and driver for Business Intelligence. It collects data from multiple source systems, transforms and melds that data into a single, integrated library of information which is accurate integrated, cleaned, reconciled and easily accessible. The resulting presentation library of information is the `single source of truth' which can be used by the organization with support and analysis, and other aspects of the analytic platform. faith in the underlying quality. The value of a well designed, effective and efficient Business Intelligence Engine cannot be overstated.

History and Rationale

The Toughest Job For decades, transaction applications have been built in relative isolation from the remainder of the organization. The result was multiple silos of transaction data. Now, a new plateau has been reached in the industry. Much of the transaction application work has been through several cycles of development. There is a recognized need to see and use the information in these silos of transaction data from across the organization. There is a large price to be paid to do this. From the many versions of the transaction data, we need to build one unified and integrated whole. How do we take those 3-4-5 or even 15 versions of individual data elements and fold them into a central information library which is integrated, unified, accurate and can provide the information needed by the organization to manage the business.

Actually, in some cases, it just cannot be accomplished. This situa-tion is one of the major reasons for failure for a Business Intelligence application. Understanding that the impossible can be encountered, recognizing it and building all the relevant implications into the Busi¬ness Intelligence development methodology is important. In most cases, however, if the data is present in the source data stores, there are ways to clean, reformat and integrate that data.

Each set of transaction data now must be reintegrated into a unified set of data for the use of the whole organization. Extract, Transform and Load systems are the answer to that dilemma. It can be truly amazing what can be done with technology, hard work, and careful analysis. The software in this arena has become increasingly auto-mated and capable.

Definition and Objectives

ETL is like the 'little engine that could'. ETL stands for Extract, Transform and Load. It is much more than data collection, transfor-mation and transfer. Although those are the basics. This Business Intelligence Engine fixes mistakes in the original data, captures that transaction data for the organization and unifies and integrates into a secure, centralized library. It creates all the documentation neces-sary to meet government regulations and organization requirements for data tracking and follow-up. It provides all the meta data and documentation necessary for use of the data as business informa-tion to leverage performance and operations improvements for the organization.

The Business Intelligence Engine and its various process stages are described in this chapter. This includes movement across the or-ganization of the Business Intelligence *product* through the various stages of transformation from the *raw data* to *information to business Intelligence.*

Platforms and Data Movement

As the data is moved across the organization infrastructures, there are certain stages and transitions which should be noted:

Sourcing - how and where is the data coming from; how effec-tive is the collection; how comprehensive;

Staging - The data staging area of the data warehouse is both a

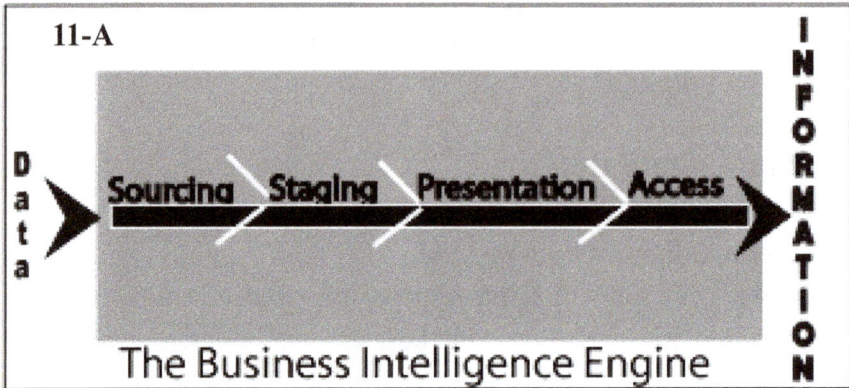

11-A

Data

Sourcing   Staging   Presentation   Access

INFORMATION

The Business Intelligence Engine

storage area and a set of processes commonly referred to as ex-tract-transformation-load (ETL). The data staging area is for the work in process and includes everything between the operational source systems and the data presentation area. This is also referred to as the back room of the data warehouse.

Presentation - This is where the data is organized, stored, and made available for direct querying by users, report writers, and other analytical applications.

Access - This is the arena which includes the interface with the users. access tools, like ad hoc reporting; query, data mining. All the data access tools available within the organization along with the other user interface components are part of this stage.

Extract, Transform and Load Functions

The Business Intelligence Engine includes the following functions:

- Design
- Document
- Operations
    1. Extract
    2. Transform
    3. Load

These functions may be provided by one of the many excellent ETL toolsets on the market today. They may also be created by developers in house, or there may be a combination of ETL vendor software and internal development software.

2. The Evolving Marketplace.

Several things are currently happening in the industry.

- The Data Warehouse has, in most cases, reached a level of demand which forces 24 x 7 operations. There is no longer a 'batch window' for update of the data.
- We are moving toward real time or near real time collec-tion of source data. Streaming data architectures for real time operational data capture and change data capture methods are a reality. (Change data capture does not require extraction of the whole of the source data base, and extraction is based on logs or other event triggers to collect only the data which has

202 Measuring Business Intelligence Success

been changed since the last pass.)

- The Extract, Transform, Load (ETL) architectures are changing. In many cases, there is a lot of competition from other types of software for the ETL functionality. For example, database management systems are building in more and more of the required ETL capabilities.

- The platform itself, i.e. the physical location for the trans-formation processing, has changed. The processing may occur on source, target or a separate platform, entirely. For higher volume operations, a separate platform is most often adopted.

- There is a growing recognition of the crucial need for meta data at all stages and in all its forms, This includes describing in detail the source conditions, the transformation logic, and other details of the processing history. This meta data is seen to be an integral part of every ETL stage, from the initial collection to the final movement into archival storage. The meta data processing and storage must be an integrated part of the Business Intelligence Engine.

3. The Audit Wheel

The basic power within the Business Intelligence Engine is the Extract, Transform, Load software and processes. We include both the core functions, as well as some expanded integration capabilities and requirements. This whole technology arena is changing rapidly. Vendors are moving quickly to respond to client requirements and to meet competitor initiatives. Performance management and integration vendor entries are further complicating and enhancing the overall potential here.

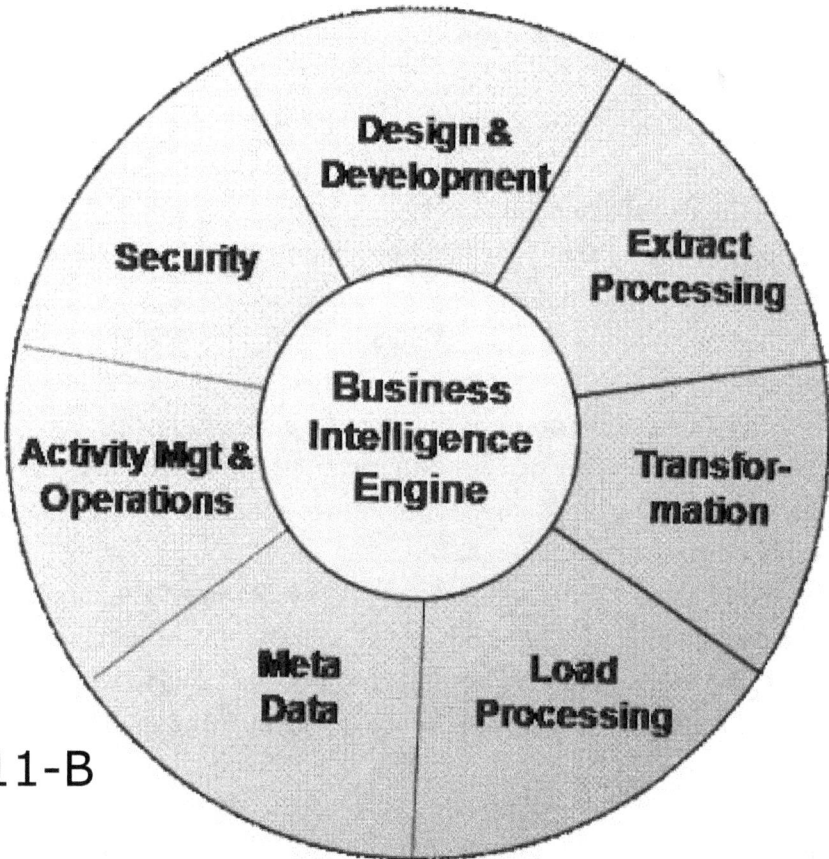

11-B

The Audit Wheel for the Business Intelligence Engine has been developed to guide the analysis and review of this arena of Business Intelligence. The Key Assessment Features are shown in the Audit Wheel in Figure 11-C. These Key Assessment Features will be described in this chapter. Audit guidelines and comments will be made where relevant to the subject.

4. Key Assessment Features

4.1. Design and Development

Defining the Requirements

The primary steps in the design and development of the ETL processing:

1. Business Requirements. We gather the business requirements
and the information needs of the users for a specific business intelligence application or application subset. These are business requirements for the Business Intelligence application - i.e. how is the business information to be used.

2. From these business requirements the details of the target databases within the Enterprise Data Warehouse are designed. These information requirements dictate the exact data to be added to the Enterprise Data Warehouse and identify the sources for that data.

Business Needs. A detailed list of all the known requirements for the business applications is compiled, checked, recompiled, and checked again. The target database which represents the requirements for Business Intelligence (the integrated data warehouse) is designed, developed and a test data base is used for testing of the basic assumptions and realities.

ETL Tools and Description

The design arena for the Business Intelligence Engine most often provides a 'user friendly' interface for the developer and it includes easy to use graphics and pictorial tools. Using this graphical environment, the developer can:

- Map source data to target data;
- Define any necessary transformations in the data;
- Detail the process flows;
- Define and Set up the operations activities

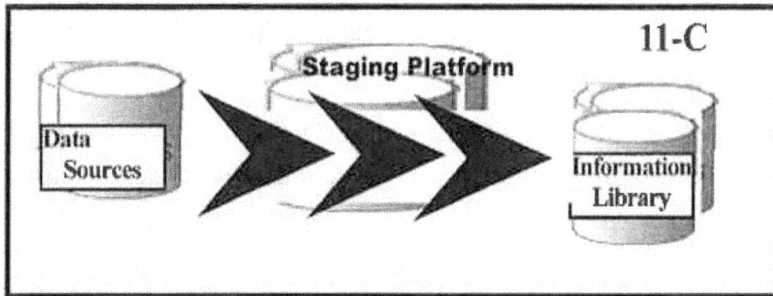

Considerations

Some of the considerations and background information which is relevant to the design and development arena are:

- The raw data will be collected, transformed and loaded into target data stores.
- These target data stores will most likely have been designed as a part of a Business Intelligence application project. A map, i.e data model, is created. (The Business Intelligence applications development methods are discussed in Chapter 16).
- The mapping process includes the selection of each data item from a graphical representation of the source data set and then identification of the matched data item within a map of the target data set.
- Any necessary transformations to the data and intermedi-ate processing steps will be identified and documented using the ETL Design tools.

· This design process also allows the definition of all jobs, operations activities and documentation requirements.

4.2 Extract Processing

Runtime processing. The data is extracted from the source data bases which have been identified and mapped during the design process. *The data extraction may be relatively straightforward and problem free. However, in most cases this is not the case. It is recommended that there be careful analysis of the source data and the source data bases well before the actual production sourcing of the Business Intelligence data is required. There can be numerous issues with the data as well as the data base structures. This could include, for example, data values which are not consistent with the definitions plus undocumented changes to the data base structures.*

The data may be extracted from the source data stores using any of the tools and platforms available within the organization. This will most likely include SQL scripting tools and adapters like ODBC (Open Data Base Connectivity.).

Extraction includes - contacting and connecting with the data source; scheduling and capturing the source data; and writing the data to temporary storage (i.e. data staging). Depending on the structure of the source, the data is usually written to flat files (for legacy data in structures like IMS and XML type data) or relational databases. Other than extraction and writing to temporary storage, the only transformation issues to be handled in this stage concern some of the low level data structures, like repeating groups and data formats.

This step of the runtime processing must be as fast and efficient as possible. Otherwise, application processing may be impacted and/or the data may not be extracted completely and efficiently.

Throughout the process, the stored data mappings from the design process are used as the guide for the extraction.

Audit Notes

The auditors should follow the trail of the developers and of the extract processing. Identify and understand the whole of the design process, the source data structures and data, and find out what kinds of problems have been encountered in the past. Some specifics and questions to be asked during the Audit Process are:

· How comprehensive is the design process and the usual design?

· Exactly what ETL tools are being used and how effective are they?

· Exactly what extract methods are being used and how effective are they?

· What kind of meta data is collected? Where is it stored? How is it accessed?

· How effective is the design? i.e. what kinds of problems occur and how persistent are they? Are the problems persistent or recurring?

· Is there always a preliminary study of the data -- well before anticipated production is required?

· How and where is the data coming from; how effective is the collection; how comprehensive?

4.3. Transformation

The Business Intelligence Engine profiles the data, looking for errors, inconsistencies and generally providing the necessary base for ensuring accuracy. It integrates the data from multiple sources and ensures that each piece of that data is checked for consistency (For example, are the names and addresses the same in every case?) This ETL Engine incorporates all the multiple data points into a single piece of data in the integrated library and ensures that it is formatted 'correctly' and labeled correctly.

Any unit of data in the Enterprise Data Warehouse has a specific name and a specific definition. Wherever the name and/or the defi-nition of any source data point is the same as the target data point in the Enterprise Data Warehouse, then the source data must be somehow translated into a form which will match the target. The definition and layout of the necessary transformation activities and steps are primary objectives of the design process. The goal of the transformation process is to take each of the multiple sources of that matching data unit and translate it 'on the fly 'to a data value which can be stored in the data warehouse.

The data to be transformed has, at this stage of processing will have been extracted from the source data stores and is now available in the Staging area of the Enterprise Data Warehouse. Most likely the first step in this process will start with data in a flat file format. The final data base storage will be a relational database in either a normalized or dimensional data base format. There may be some transformations which are requisite to making the data suitable for these data base structures. This will have been part of the ETL design process.

Cleaning of the data includes - ensuring unified structures and properties; enforcing rules for the data and values, as well as the business rules; building the detailed meta data to describe the data and the transformations. Data cleaning steps can be complex and may be automated with double checks by computer/human combinations. Some of examples of data cleaning are:

· values - presence, validity, consistency - i.e. addresses
· duplicate data -- does a customer exist more than once - with, for example, slightly different attributes
· business rule compliance

Data Integration. The data mapping for the ETL processes occurs after the design process and provides an integrated database design, or model, which describes how the data will be stored. The data is mapped to the proper location within the integrated database, as defined in that design process. Data integration means ensuring that a single version and only a single version for the same piece of data exists. If there are differences which cannot be reconciled, then that data is considered separate and named as a separate piece of data.
This means that, since the data is coming from multiple data sources, there are some required housekeeping and conforming steps. Queries cannot be made unless there is an integration of the data. The textual labels must be identical and the measures must be rationalized. This data conformation is the result of a lot of up front work in terms of agreements by the users related to the definitions and design of the data. Any special indexing and other query features will be struc-tured in the database and any checks for operability should be done in preliminary design phases.

Audit Notes

The primary guidelines are as noted above for the Extract process. Follow *the requirements. See how the design is accomplished and how* it ties in to the runtime processing. Make sure that all the necessary meta data is captured (see the Meta Data Key Assessment Feature in later section.). Identify any specific issues or problems.

4.4 Load

The transformed data is stored as the final form in the Staging, i.e. working, arena, of the Enterprise Data Warehouse. It is ready to be loaded into the target data stores of the Presentation Library. The formats of the target data stores are relational data bases with a normalized data base or dimensional data base structure. The target data models have been described in the design model and the appropriate data has been mapped. The data may be loaded using SQL scripts or bulk loaders - which will insert or modify the data values in the target data stores.

Delivering - The last step is to structure the data and load it into the final database for presentation, i.e. the library of information which can be used by the business intelligence analytical applications and end users. For the Kimball data warehouse, the final database structure is dimensional, i.e. based on star schema models with facts and dimension tables. Although there is some dispute over whether some of these steps are 'back room' processing or 'front room', this is more related to the type of data warehouse and the data model rather than the nature of the processing. In every case, the data must go through each of the primary steps. In the case of the Inmon style data warehouse, with its first level normalized data base with follow-on aggregates, two sets of ETL processing may be required.

Audit Guidelines
Note the forms of the data which are sources and targets for the load process. Check the comprehension of the documentation within the ETL Toolset(s). There should, most likely, be some additional documentation, which describes the flow and movement of the data and *formats of the intermediate data stores.*

4.5 Meta Data

There should be a meta data repository associated with the ETL software. This repository should parallel all the activities within ETL design, development and production. Comprehensive meta data must be collected at every stage - from design through archiving through runtime activities. That means that all target mapping through the actual collection, transformation and load of the data values must be captured in the meta data library. All the audit information needs to be collected, including such meta data as, relevant times of extraction and movement, any identification of data stewards, and complete information about where the data is stored and what are the intermediate and final forms.

This meta data should be accessible to the Business Intelligence Engine throughout the process. All the meta data must also be available to rest of the system, both Business Intelligence and other information technology systems through easy to access interfaces.

Audit Guidelines
The meta data of the Business Intelligence Engine is critical to all the other parts of the Business Intelligence Asset Base. The importance of collecting, storing and sharing of this information cannot be overstated.

Identify what meta data is being collected. How is it being stored? Is it updated in parallel with the data design and processing? Is it in a form which can be easily understood and accessed by other systems, programs and users? Is the meta data used? How and in what other areas of the Business Intelligence Asset Base is it most critical?

4.5 Activity Management and Operations

This is a combined subject area which includes all the infrastructure and operational activities associated with the Business Intelligence Engine. The software of the engine, i.e. the ETL software and in some cases combined with additional operational infrastructures of the organization, includes the necessary components to accomplish the following.

· Utilities and Job Structuring and Processing - technical administrators schedule the ETL jobs, run and monitor them. The stan-dard protocols and processes apply. The jobs are monitored, events are logged, and if there are nay problems, then there are recovery and restart and data reconciliation procedures. The major operational functions are:
· job scheduling
· job execution
· exception handling
· recovery and restart
· quality checking
· release
· support

(It has been noted in another chapter that the streaming data requirements for real time data capture is most often considered an entirely different paradigm. For one thing, even the collection of source data is different, in that the data may actually be 'pushed' into the data information collection area, based on events or value changes.)

· Meta data management - There is a meta data repository which stores and manages all the information about the design and run-time process. This meta data is accessed and used throughout the design and runtime stages of the ETL processing. This meta data is crucial. See the notes in the previous section.

· The extraction process, as noted above, consults the meta data repository management system to identify the data to be extracted. The extraction is handled using available organization system infrastructure tools, e.g. ODBC or SQL or other adapters.

· Loading of the data is managed using SQL scripts, data adapters, or bulk loaders - to insert and update the target data in the Enterprise Data Warehouse - i.e. the presentation library data stores

· Movement of the data - tools and software use the common file protocols and networks in use within the organization to move data into and out of the data stores and memory caches.

Some Notes about the Processing

A few points about the process should be made here:

· Query should not be allowed in any of the staging databases or processing areas. There are a number of reasons for this - including the fact that the data is not fully prepared and the 'back room processing' should not be burdened with the additional work of ensuring that the data is prepared to be queried, security issues, etc.

· There is not necessarily a single flow of data within the back room processing. There can be parallel and embedded operations.

· Data may be collected which is not required in the current Business Intelligence Presentation library. In some cases, e.g. for compliance or archival reasons, this extraneous data may be saved in auxiliary databases.

Data Latency. This term refers to the requirements for delivery of the data to the end user. As has been mentioned in other parts of this book - the industry has been moving toward the idea of 'near real time to real time' presentation of the business information. Most often the organization will be using batch processing for collection of the data for the data warehouse. This processing can be speeded up and made very acceptable for even 24 x 7 operations of the data warehouses and for most needs for historical data. However, when an organization develops a real time or near real time business intelligence applica¬tion - then the whole of the Business Intelligence Engine structure and processing changes. This would be an entirely separate set of processes - either replacing the batch collection system or in addition to it. Most likely, there would be a separate arena for the organization and the drivers and inherent requirements might be altogether different. This 'real time' arena should be audited as a separate entity and clear definitions sought for requirements and objectives. Any audit should be based on those definitions and requirements.

4.6 Security & Compliance

Compliance Requirements. Government requirements for tracking and auditing of data are more strict now than ever. ETL processing is one of the Business Intelligence Asset Base components which should have logical points to ensure that all the data has the associated meta data and tracking mechanisms to be able to provide for these requirements. Depending on the organization, the industry and the specific requirements, any audit of ETL will have to include a detailed review of these requirements and how they are being met.

Security Requirements. Data security is of crucial importance to an organization for many reasons, including proprietary information and customer safety reasons. Data security is also a government mandated requirement for many industries, like health care. However, everything about the data warehouse is focused on providing readily available, easy to access information. So security may be low in priority for ETL data processing.

Within the ETL arena, the primary audit for security should be an identification of the exact security needs and a review of any security activities in the design and processing. There should be a check to ensure that the organization is using role based security systems, which means that access to the data is defined by what role the person plays within the organization. If there is a different security method, then there should be further analysis of that method. However, the other major concerns for audit of the security aspects of the ETL processing go more to the vetting of the people involved and the lock down and tracking of the physical data materials, like tapes and files. A major item for the auditor to check is the availability of a documented data security program. Where is it? What is in it?

Meta data is equally important. The meta data for the Business Intelligence applications must include all the information about the data. That includes any security notes, audit information, as well as data stewards and certification meta data. Because the data may be rolled off the active data stores within the Enterprise Data Warehouse, there must be some method of tracking, auditing, and securing the data.

Audit Notes

Find out how the data security is handled. How is the tracking and auditing of the data handled? If the data is archived or channeled off the active production stores during the processing- identify the method for securing the data in the alternate data paths.

5. Audit Guidelines

A primary reason for auditing the Business Intelligence Engine is to get an overall picture of the movement of data across the organization. We should be auditing each of the components and the infrastructures - as part of other audit segments. With the Business Intelligence Engine, we want to get a good picture of the overall design and management of the data movement. Is it seamless? Are there major arterial clogs where data seems always to have translation or movement issues? For this audit, we should follow some data clusters and try to identify where they are coming from and how they are getting from point to point.

Some of the points which should be identified and rated are:
- Data

  1 Extract - speed, efficiency, low level data format and other translations

  2.   Clean - speed, effectiveness, product results, manual intervention requirements

  3.   Integrate - data model/database categories, integration results, one from many processing

  4.   Load - much of the complexity related to data load processing may be in the modeling of the database.
- Operations - execution, performance, capabilities for restart/ recovery, speed, effectiveness, efficiency.

· Associated

    · Documentation - Full documentation of process-es, infrastructures and toolsets; full documentation of all processes, like near-line and archiving operations (which may be considered as completely separate func-tions)

    · Meta data - full technical meta data for all extrac-tion sources, transformations, and associated is-sues encountered. Full audit flow information.

    · Front Room/Back Room delineations - No query operations should be allowed in the back room staging areas - if so -- then the 'back room processing' area be-comes essentially a secondary presentation library with all the requirements for security, query formatting; ap-ply.

    · Security - check administration and lock down of disks, tapes, paper documents. Government and propri-etary requirements for data security mandate physical security of areas for processing. Data security for disk internals is most often covered with rule based security systems. Check what these are and how effective.

    · Streaming vs Batch - Has the organization moved to a whole new paradigm of streaming data and if so, check on success of operations flow and which data impacted.

    · Pre operations - data profiling and tested data and procedures - Although not actually a part of the opera-tional aspects of data integration, the success and effi-ciency is impacted by the preliminary design, data pro-filing and testing to ensure that the data being extracted is accurate. Was the data profiled for accuracy and proof of concept testing accomplished pre operations?

Rate the Data Flow Processing and the Operations separately.

Capability Maturity Rating

The audit points to be reviewed and the Competency ratings to be applied are:

· Level 1 - If the Data Integration Platform is not an enterprise wide environment - then the rating should 0 or 1. Whether 0 or 1 should be dependent on how well any independent data marts are integrating data for their applications.

· Rating of 2 - 3 and 4: Organization recognizes the need for a data integration platform; the foundation architecture is in place for an data warehouse; There may also be some integration of data through federation means rather than standard ETL practices as included in this chapter. Rate the Business Intelligence Engine in the early stages of development based on completeness of process¬ing for those applications included; successful implementation and extensions of the data library; and measurements for speed and performance. Speed and performance, data accuracy and integration, and capabilities in loading of presentation databases should be rated. Rate on judged level of competency - 2-3-4 for each of the factors.

· Level 5 - This Maturity level includes all the capabilities to meet an optimized Data Integration Platform success level, as well as the one or more of the following:

> · the capabilities for streaming data
> · Service Oriented enterprise Architecture interfaces
> · structured as well as unstructured data
> · enterprise centralized meta data repository

11-D

	KEY PERFORMANCE INDICATORS															
Rate each Key Assessment Feature for each of the KPI's. Rating should be 1 to 5, with 5 as hightest rating. See the appropriate chapter for audit and rating guidelines	Mangement	Support	BUSINESS	ALGNMNT	PARTNER	SHIP	Business	Goals	Scalabil	INTEGRA TION	ADAPT	ABILITY	PERFORM ANCE	USER FRIENDLY	COMPRE HENSION	QUALITY	VALUE
Design & Development																
Extract Processing																
Transformation																
Load Processing																
Meta Data																
, Operations																
Security																
Business Intelligence Engine																

Key Assessment Features

12

Technical Infrastructure

Chapter Contents

1. Introduction

The Technical Infrastructure provides the framework, the foundation and transportation systems for Business Intelligence Data. These components must be in place or nothing works. This technical infrastructure is the first layer of the Business Intelligence architecture. It is the underlying technical environment on which the remainder of Business Intelligence is built. The technical infrastruc ture includes: hardware, middleware, operating systems, networks, database and meta data management systems and installed vendor product software. The vendor software includes everything from the middleware or messaging infrastructure to the Extract, Transform and Load (ETL) engine as well as the database, meta data engine, data cleansing engines, schedulers, and so on. All the components of this technical infrastructure should be well selected and adapted to match the business intelligence requirements of the organization. However, too often, the infrastructure has been constructed over time and the parts and architecture have not been focused on meeting the specific needs for Business Intelligence.

2. The Audit Wheel

The Key Assessment Features have been identified and can be seen in the Audit Wheel, Figure 12-A. Each of the Key Assessment Features is defined and described in the remainder of the chapter. Audit notes and assessment guidelines are included both in the section re-

12-A

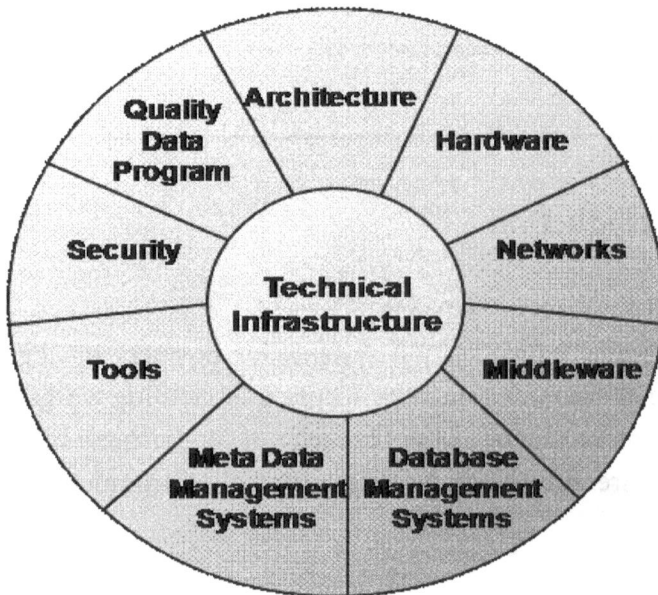

lated to each feature and in the summary section, Audit Guidelines.

3. Key Assessment Features

The Key Assessment Features of the Technical Infrastructure are identified in the Audit Wheel in figure 12-A. Data and Meta data are the work products and are considered separately from either the technical or non technical infrastructures.

3.1 Architectures

(I would like to thank Carnegie Mellon and the information on their web site for much of the information in this section. The web site is www.sei.cmu.edu Any mistakes are my own.)

Computer and system architectures have changed consistently and sometimes dramatically over the last few decades. The Service Oriented Architecture which is in an initial stage of introduction and change today is derived from and represents a form of the client server architectures in place since before 1990. In this section, we will describe some of the various architectures which have been used and are in use today. This discussion should provide a foundation for understanding the parts of the technical infrastructure, e.g. the hardware, middleware, networks, Where possible, some of the advantages to specific systems are identified.

The predominant architecture in middle to large scale organizations today is client-server. Some of the recent architectures are described below:

Mainframe Architecture. With mainframe architectures, all intel-ligence is in the central host computer. The user interacts with the central computer through terminals. Terminals may be PC's or workstations. In the current industry environment, mainframes have come to be used more and more as large scale file servers in distributed - client/server environments. Mainframes with terminals could not accommodate the upsurge in graphical user interfaces.

File sharing architecture. (PC/LAN) In this architecture, the file is downloaded from the server to the user work environment. Then the job is run - with both data and logic - in the local, desk top, environment. This works only for very small amounts of data, and a small number of users.

In the 1990's the PC LAN environment changed, pushed by ever larger numbers of users and the popularity of graphical user interfaces.

Client Server architecture is a versatile, message based, modular infrastructure that is intended to improve usability, flexibility, seal-ability, and interoperability as compared with the older centralized, mainframe, timesharing computer systems. A client is defined as a requestor of services. A Server is defined as the provider of services. A single machine can be both a client and a server, depending on the software configuration.

Client server architecture. The limitations in the file server architecture pushed the introduction and use of the client server architecture. A database server replaced the file server. With a Data Base Management System, queries for data can be answered directly -rather than sending the whole file to the application. This reduces network traffic and also allows for multi-user update and access through a GUI front end. The language for communication between the client and server uses either remote procedure calls (RPC) or standard query language (SQL)

There may be two tier systems with a user system in local desktop machines and database management services in a server which is more powerful and handles many clients. This two tier configuration is most suitable for a smaller number of clients.

The three tier architecture for client servers emerged to solve the restrictions imposed by the two tier model. A middle tier is added between the user and the server. This middle tier can perform queuing, application processing, and database staging. This allows the client and server to be able to deliver messages to the middle tier, then disengage. The middle tier handles scheduling and prioritization. This three tier approach provides the flexibility and capacities needed for large scale systems.

Types of middle layer:

Transaction Processing Monitor technology -- this is a type of message queuing, transaction, scheduling and prioritization. The client connects to the TP monitor (in the middle layer) and the TP monitor takes over scheduling and managing the request. To be most effective this middle layer is usually handled by third party vendor software and can manage large numbers of users. In some smaller cases, the middle layer could be handled by the data base management systems - but this is not as effective and service is rapidly degraded with number of users and volumes.

This middle layer - or TP monitor also provides for
·   the ability to update multiple different databases in a single transaction
·   transaction prioritizing
·   capability for connection to a variety of different data sources - e.g. flat files, non relational dbms and the mainframe

This architecture is scalable and cost effective for large systems.

Three Tier Client Server Architecture with messaging - Messaging is another way to implement three tier architectures. The messages are
·   prioritized
·   processed asynchronously
·   consist of headers and the message. The header contains address and id numbers and any priority info.

The *three tier architecture with messaging* places intelligence in the messages. The TP monitor technology has the intelligence in the monitor and just transports 'dumb' messages.

Three tier client server - with application server. The application is run mainly on a shared host. The application server does not drive the GUI - but it shares logic, computations and a data retrieval engine. With this approach there is less logic on the client machine. There is also less security on the client to worry about. The application is more scalable, and support and maintenance costs are much lower. Essentially there is only the single server to maintain rather than many desk top, local, clients. Cost, scalability and security are best served with this architecture.

Three tier with an ORB architecture. This is an evolving tech-nology which supports distributed objects. The architecture allows for independence from language, Operating Systems, and technology based implementation requirements. This extends the distrib-uted object technologies. The distributed objects support interoper-ability across languages and platforms and enhance maintainability and adaptability of the system. Two current examples are CORBA - Common Object Request Broker and COM/DCOM - component object model. The industry association, Object Mapping Group (OMG), has supplied the mapping necessary to relate the two.

Distributed/Collaborative enterprise architecture. This architecture is based on the ORB architecture, but extends it by using shared, reusable components consisting of business models (not just objects) across the enterprise. This combines the standardized business object with distributed object computing. Instead of the limited messages of prior architectures, the intermediate products are full objects, which are essentially contained 'systems', or business models. These contained reusable business models provides much more flexibility. The potential of the concepts is tremendous. This is the foundation for Service Oriented Architectures.

Service Oriented Architectures. This architecture is a major step forward involving the concepts and technologies for distributed processing and modular programming. The unit for distribution is called a service. These services are larger, self contained units which are to be distributed across the network, i.e. between client and server. These services are very small function groups, usually of some larger set of functions, (i.e. what might have been coded into an application program in pre-services technology). Such a service might be to place an order, or pay a bill. Services are relatively large objects or units for specific functions which are self contained. These services are sent, then mapped together, or orchestrated, by a receiver. This architecture should allow for much more flexibility, and for costs to go down, since an organization only needs to develop or purchase exactly those services which meets their requirements. This is a major jump forward over the initial data object which was the initial basketball for the client server technology.

3.2 Hardware

Definition. The Hardware Key Assessment Feature of the Business Intelligence Technical Infrastructure includes all the basic computer machinery, from work stations to servers and any other boxes which are part of the platform. Computer hardware is the physical part of a computer.

Hardware Characteristics.
Consistent and stable environment. The hardware of a computer system is relatively consistent and stable. This may be contrasted with the software tools which are usually more easily migrated in and out of the infrastructure base. It is fairly common for the hardware platform to have been built slowly, over time. The requirements for each selection have, most likely, been dictated by the environment at the time of purchase. This sometimes makes for a disparate collection, which is not necessarily the best overall infrastructure for Business Intelligence.

Power. The hardware must have sufficient power to handle com¬plex access and analysis requirements against large volumes of data. It has to support not only predefined, simple queries on summary data, but also ad hoc complex queries on detailed data.

The term 'power' refers essentially to speed and size requirements. At the 'front-end', the technical infrastructure which supports the Data Warehouse Presentation Library, including associated data marts, it is critical to provide for plenty of power to ensure satisfactory performance. Query and report performance and other similar user interface activities demand rapid response and delivery of data.

The 'back room' processing of the Data Warehouse refers to the parts of the platform where the data is extracted, transformed and integrated and loaded into the Presentation Library. Computing strength is also important here. However, the performance issues (for a Data Warehouse which contains only historical data) may not be so time critical. However, as the organization moves toward more real time data availability, this `back room' power and responsiveness moves up on the priority scale.

Scalable. The hardware must be scalable, i.e. easily upgraded to meet new requirements. The hardware platform must be flexible and easily upgraded to handle changes in data volumes, data updates, access patterns. The hardware platform must also be able to accommodate changes and fast growth in interface and access of the Business Intelligence data - e.g. number of people, reports & analytical activity, tools, and the systems interfaces. If new hard-ware is added 'on the fly', then the system must be able to use it to improve performance.

Audit notes. Identifying the hardware within the Business Intelligence environment is a first step in the audit process. Everything which is part of the infrastructure which supports and/or impacts the Data Integration Platform and the Analytics Platform should be identified and reviewed. This can be accomplished by listing the expected functions and requirements for Business Intelligence and correlating these with the available hardware. There should be extensive documentation for the systems and run time operational statistics.

During any audit of the technical infrastructure, the following questions should be addressed:

- What hardware are we using for Business Intelligence? Is there enough staff to maintain and support all of it?
- Do we have enough hardware for our data and user re-quirements?
- How scalable it the hardware and how rapidly can it be up-graded?
- Does the hardware perform as an integrated whole?

Capacity and Growth Capabilities
What are we looking at? Servers, workstations, operating systems, and associated technologies. What are we looking for? Assessing the hardware requires reviewing the planning, capacity and other documentation and it means talking with the technical architecture engineers, capacity planners and the Business Intelligence planners and managers. How much growth in data and user volumes have been planned for? Have the Business Intelligence planners kept the engineers informed? Have the engineers been an integral part of all required meetings, etc. Is there a team of business and technology staff with the responsibility for planning and managing the technology, including the hardware?

In many cases, the growth within the Business Intelligence arena may have been piecemeal and chaotic. There should be some responsible group or individual or even just a set of documentation which shows an enterprise understanding and the directives for management of the overall Business Intelligence Asset Base. The assessment of hardware for the Business Intelligence Asset Base should identify whether there is such an understanding and also how effective it is. Are there staff members whose job it is to assess and plan for growth - to monitor performance? In many cases, hardware assessment takes place after the fact, when it is self-evident that there is 'not enough'; when performance has already eroded and the system has turned to molasses. Look for evidence and anecdotal experiences. There should be management software, logs and other systems documentation. Find out what is available, ask for it and review it carefully.

Key Performance Indicators. Review the organization hardware using each of the relevant Key Performance Indicators (see Chapter 8)

3.3 Networks

Networks include all the communications, interface and sharing resources involved in the organization's computer systems. (A network is usually defined as *two or more computers connected together us-ing a telecommunication system for the purpose of communicating and sharing resources. The devices can be separated by a few feet through Local Area Networks, or thousands of miles through Wide Area Networks. A wide area network (WAN) is a computer network that covers a broad geographical area. This is usually a network that uses routers and public communications links. The internet is essentially a large WAN. A computer network is any set of computers or devices connected to each other. (NOTE; Thank you to WIKIPEDIA - a great website. We love you - the site and everyone who contributes, whoever and wherever you are.)*

The major relevance to an assessment project or to the Business Intelligence Asset Base becomes evident only when the network structure does NOT work. Does the system provide the basic functions required? Also, and this is the principal question for analysis of the infrastructure ---

> **Is there enough bandwidth to provide for current requirements and for rapid, high volume growth?**

For assessment purposes, we ask similar questions to the same specialists as noted under the hardware components. The network architecture should be essentially transparent to developers and users. However, those charged with making sure that the system is scalable and flexible will need to know who to talk with and who will decide how much band width and what kinds of communications infrastructure are required. The communication engineers will be able to ascertain how much and what is needed. They also know if organization has what it needs.

Some specific questions for these engineers, during the audit, is what kinds of data, what volumes of data, how many users and what categories of users are they planning for in their projections for their systems and platforms. If there is no documentation and they don't know or do not have the information readily available - there may be a problem. This area may need further evaluation, at any rate. Advice to the auditor: **Seek until they know.**

3.4 Middleware

Middleware is a term which describes a piece of software that connects two or more software applications so that they can exchange data. Middleware is the runtime software layer which lies between the operating system and the applications. **Middleware** acts a bridge for integration of the application programs and other software in the arena of client/server architectures and complex networked architectures in a distributed computing environment.

The Middleware should support:
- ...directory services,
- ...message-passing mechanisms;
- ...and specifically - database gateways.

A directory service is software which stores and organizes information about a computer network's users and network resources. It allows network administrators to manage users' access to the resources.

Most Middleware falls into one of the following categories:

> ·...Data Management Middleware - this connects an application or DBMS on one platform with a DBMS running on another platform;
> ·...Distributed logic middleware - this middleware supports program to program communication between two pieces of custom written code.

Large organizations will often have a middleware or messaging infrastructures such as IBM Websphere MQ, Microsoft BizTalk, Tibco or Oracle Fusion Middleware.

Data Management middleware includes database gateways. Database gateways give end users a way to access information stored in disparate databases. To house the mountains of information they generate, large corporations today rely on a wide range of database management systems (DBMSs). These databases most often use proprietary technology. This means that in order to provide access to the data in these databases, organizations add in a layer of software that identifies and translates DBMS differences.

These database management gateways are required to connect the various network architectures of desktops, other clients and servers to the enterprise main servers. There are four major categories:

> ·...point to point - which provide access to a single type of data base management system
> ·...universal - which provide general access across a set of platforms
> ·...SQL - provides access to relational databases - the gateway translates the request into native SQL used by the server's rela-tional database.
> ·...ODBC type gateways - (open database connectivity) - these are based on vendor specifications.

Database drivers (DLL) link applications to the database management system.

For the assessment and rating of the organization capability in this area, the analyst should ensure that the middleware being used is at least industry standard and provides for performance and efficiency for data movement through the system. Essentially, the issue is: Do we have the middleware necessary to retrieve the operational data from multiple different platforms; transfer it into our Business Intelligence environment then to provide the necessary movement through that environment?

3.5 Database Management Systems

A database management system (DBMS) is computer software designed for the purpose of managing databases. Typical examples of DBMSs include Oracle, Microsoft SQL Server, MySQL, DB2.

The database management infrastructure includes not only the Database Management System, but also the software and hardware which move the data between the application and the data storage.

Perhaps the single most critical set of components in providing for performance of Business Intelligence systems are the underlying database management systems. Database management platforms may range from local file servers in isolation to workgroup/server structures to full blown enterprise wide and/or mainframe type platforms. Size and requirements for the DBMS infrastructure are dictated by the requirements of the Business Intelligence organization, including short and long term projections. A single data mart application might be satisfied with a local file server - e.g. with a desktop database. An organization with this type of basic DBMS platform, exclusively, should be rated at a Maturity Level of 1. Larger applications may require a workgroup type of structure with a relational database management system for a small group of users and applications. An enterprise wide system of a complex, encompassing Business Intelligence Asset Base will require heavy duty, high volume relational data base hardware and software.

Database management systems have been available for a long time in the industry. The Very Large Scale Database Management Systems are complex and amazing to contemplate in their sheer responsiveness and capabilities.

There are other features of a database management system which are specific to the requirements for Business Intelligence. Some of these are: Aggregation and summary data; dimensional data mart - star schemas; recognition of the types of data structures and automated, integrated processing of these particular structures; partitioning and bitmap indexing and other specialized indexing schemes; materialized views and advanced query optimization and processing; transparent performance enhancements for sort, aggregation and other important Business Intelligence Operations.

In fact, what we need to look for from the Business Intelligence perspective are mostly well thought out capabilities which will do the jobs necessary and provide high speed performance. Understanding and assessing these capabilities is critical to a successful Business Intelligence Asset Base. In most cases the vendors of these data base management systems have anticipated and built in tremendous numbers of services and capabilities which address all the Business Intelligence requirements. In fact, many are moving into areas which compete with other vendor arenas, like ETL. However, keep in mind that your organization is probably suffering, if some of the specific features are missing which should be available to give you the performance boost needed for your applications performance or allow your particular set of Business Intelligence tools to function well. Also, if your organization has succumbed to the newer additions to the marketplace of the Business Intelligence appliances, (i.e. 'boxes' which include the Data Base Management system - hardwired) the auditor should carefully review the list of specific expectations for the Data Base Management System. Since, at this time, appliances are newer on the market, there may be 'bugs' to be fixed and enhancements which need to be made. Look for bugs or missing features which the organization needs. As usual, the best way to find out is to ask those within the organization who are using the appliance.

Audit and Assessment: When do we need more DBMS power and storage. The assessments we should be making for our Business Intelligence Capability Model are: Does the organization have the expertise to make the proper decisions? Is there a documented and in-place process and team of experts reviewing performance statistics and continually determining whether more power and storage are needed? The auditor should review the statistics with the organization experts and assess their process and resources for ensuring that there is enough power for peak loads, for 24 hour production/online operations, and for handling, offline, all the back up and restore.

The Key Performance Indicators are discussed in more detail in Chapter 8. Some of the Key Performance Indicators which are of particular interest in the DBMS for Business Intelligence requirements are discussed below.

Assessing features for the Database Management System and whether the organization has the 'best' of the marketplace is a question for the experts. The organization needs to determine what their Business Intelligence requirements are and select a solution which is cost effective and meets those requirements.

Following are many of the features and Key Performance Indicators which the database management system should address.
   · Scalability -- Planning should provide for rapid changes in: data volumes; data update frequencies; data access patterns; # reports/queries; BI users; Toolset Access volumes; operational

data feeds. DBMS capabilities should be planned for and accommodated with all these factors in mind

· Dimensional Support - focused support for star schema models, data loading and use

· Aggregation Support - fast, easy load and use of pre-compiled summaries and aggregations of data. (Summaries are added numerics; aggregates differ slightly, in that several different fields may be grouped and made additive.)

· Archiving Support - There should be a comprehensive system of support for the ʿroll-offʾ of data from the active information library, based on age and use. This should include an automated process, including predefined triggers and transfer of data to inactive storage.

· Support for dating and other audit information - auto-matic collection and marking of data with dates, times and other information for data movement and changes.

· Support and Administration - All the standard and not so standard features - unattended operations; audit and tracking; workload tracking and tuning mechanisms; monitoring of resources, users, data volumes; preset triggers for user warnings for things like resource overloads.

· Triggers and stored procedures - Event driven, automatic (by the DBMS) running of prestored code - by data element and event.

· Resource limits and alerts - There should be user com-munications related to timing of queries, etc. if over preset limits of resources and times.

· Workload tracking and load balancing and management - close monitoring, reporting, for integration of performance and automated realignment of resources, as necessary.

· Location Transparency - Wherever the data is located in the system, users should not have to be involved in any way.

· Performance - How well and fast are queries and analytical applications handled - i.e. this may depend on degree of parallelism and other factors.

· Normalized as well as Dimensional Data Structures
· Advanced indexing - special index schemes for perfor-mance enhancement
Internet support - Many of the analytical toolsets are in-ternet based. How well does the DBMS interact?

Multiple Platforms - Should be able to house the DBMS on multiple heterogeneous platforms, i.e. Business Intelligence systems may include various sized data stores (usually data marts) on multiple platforms.
· Coordination with other hardware - software, e.g. other DBMS.
· Operations. 24 hour production/operations - with some sort of double back up and fault tolerance features; Checkpoint, re-start, recovery internals;
· Scaling --- Effective cacheing and sharing of data to mini-mize bottlenecks; multiple parallel tasking; multiple processor compatibility
· Security system - comprehensive - with fully restricted ac-cess to views, table, and data elements.
· Meta data - interfaces and collection and communica-tions with meta data repositories.
Any audit should include a review of the database management sys¬tem, the staff and the support and maintenance processes to deter¬mine how well the organization handles the issues. Although there should be some assessment of the architecture and the specific tradeoffs made with the organization DBMS - still the ultimate test is `how well does it work'? Has it handled the work load changes and what is the prognosis for tomorrow? Have there been degradations in performance?

Performance - How fast and how responsive for both the loading of the source data and the retrieval for user, i.e. timing of sending of query and return of the business information to the user. There are

a number of features which are key here ---
- · the degree of parallelism in handling queries and data loads. The DBMS manufacturers have performed mira¬cles in the area
- · advanced indexing schemas
- · use of parallel processing in handling queries and for data loading
- · clustering servers and databases

Scalability. In order to be considered scalable, a database must be able to take advantage of additional resources (memory and proc-es-sors). The computer may be a small single processor system or at the other end of the spectrum. If more memory or processors are thrown at it, the DBMS should be able to recognize and use the extras to improve performance and throughput. Scalability is the capability of handling growing amounts of work automatically and transparently, i.e. the system can be readily enlarged. If performance improves after adding hardware, (keeping everything else, like services, steady) then the organization has a scalable system. Of course, it is not quite that simple. But, on the whole, that is what defines scalable for the database management system. For example, a scalable database management system is one that can be upgraded to process more transactions by adding new processors, devices and storage. It should allow for easy, transparent upgrades without shutting down the system. Some methods being used by DBMS vendors to optimize scalability include powerful data compression features, grids or clusters of servers; Oracle states that their extensive parallel processing is at the heart of its scalability. Not only is parallelism central to query processing, it plays a key role in ETL tasks.

Database scalability is a long thought over and debated topic, and there are no easy answers. There are several ways to achieve greater scalability out of the organization's database, however the chosen architecture should fit the needs of the organization. When it comes to scalability, there seem to be two ways to achieve it -- scaling up or scaling out. Scaling up is to handle volume on a single high performance server, while scaling out is to distribute load among many lower cost servers. When scaling up you add processors to your server, when scaling out, you add servers to your cluster.

Scalability also refers to capabilities for
- expanding the capability of the data base and database management system to process and store records - i.e. storage space and processing performance.
- 24X7 availability. With continuing globalization, most large organizations require that their Business Intelligence systems be available on a continuous basis. So modification should not require 'bringing down' the system.

3.6. Meta Data Management Systems

Industry environment and practices today have not evolved to the point of a common industry recognition of the need for a centralized meta data management system. Meta data is embedded in multiple tools sets, from ETL drivers to CASE tools. Meta data is incorporated and plays a major role in the services objects in Service Oriented Architectures. In fact, the use of meta data is common.

In assessing the organization meta data resources, the audit team should research and evaluate based on the following criteria:
- Level 1: The organization meta data is limited to that which is embedded in the toolsets and various services and applications requirements.
- Level 2: There is some mechanism for interfacing the meta data among some of the various tools and applications.
- Level 3: There is a mechanism for making the meta data visible, and accessing and using any of the meta data in the Business Intelligence Asset Base.
- Level 4: There is a strong connectivity among all the points, or nodes, which contain meta data. All the meta data in the system is 'visible' and can be accessed. The access is universal

and users can see and use the meta data through search engines or similar toolsets.

· Level 5: A strong, centralized meta data library exists which allows for interconnectivity and visibility of all meta data in the system. This library includes a creation, update and management system which allows users and developers to access and update the meta data. There is universal access to the meta data and the management system. In addition, there is a strong, monitored and well managed system for creation and governance of techni-cal and business meta data. This includes the development and support for a business language repository.

12-B

Business Intelligence Tools
Development CASE Data Integration (e.g. ETL) Analytical Query & Reporting OLAP Dashboard & Scorecard Planning - Modeling Statistics & Data Mining Production Reporting

3.7 Business Intelligence Tools

As the organization matures in the Business Intelligence arena, the selection and use of the Business Intelligence tools should become more standardized and the responsibility for selection and support should be at the enterprise level.

In this chapter, the most prevalent types of tools which should be considered as part of the Business Intelligence arena are identified. These tools are described. Some considerations are discussed related to why the organization needs them; standardization issues; and assessment points.

The primary sets of tools required for Business Intelligence can be described by the requirements to be met (figure 12-C):

Development. These are tools used by the developers and creators of the Business Intelligence data structures and analytical applications.

This includes toolsets for:
  · creating the logical and physical models, (like ERwin) and those to extract and
  · create the information libraries (ETL).

The data modeling tools are used during the development phases of the application most heavily - to create the normalized and the dimensional models which are necessary to the Business Intelligence analytical tools.

The Extract, Transform, Load activities in building and supporting Business Intelligence systems takes more time than any other. Probably at least 60% of the time and resources go into the planning and data extraction, cleaning, unifying and integration of the data. There are a number of tools which are necessary for these tasks - including the basic ETL, plus special data cleansing software, and others.

Analytical. The Analytical toolsets are used by both the developers and the end users to access the data warehouse presentation library and data marts. These vary tremendously in their nature and capabilities. In some, if not most, organizations, many sets of tools are in use by various groups. This is especially true for the query and reporting tools. The desktop versions of spreadsheets and probably desktop database tools are major players in the initial stages for data mart development. In many cases, use proliferates to the point of chaos. Assessment should include identifying all the analytical tools and where they are being used, as well as the users of the tools.

What are the costs associated with the unrestrained proliferation of these tools? At any rate, there may be a need for more than a single toolset across the organization for such functions as query, reporting and OLAP. Of course, some of the other tools are very specific to the type of analytical processing to be accomplished. Review the chapter on the analytics platform for more information.

· Query and Reporting - Extract, format and present the information.
· Production Reporting - Reports are developed (frequently by Information Technology developers) and made avail¬able to the general user population on a regular basis - either through 'push' via e-mail or user access via the web or enterprise portal.
· Dashboard and Scorecard - Some of these may be in-corporated into the primary toolsets in use. There may also be some specialized tools. This is particularly true for process oriented manufacturing cultures, which have been more accustomed to the dashboard capabilities in their manufacturing facilities.
· Planning - Modeling tools - These simulation and forecasting tools allow management to ask questions, like `what if'.
· Statistics and Data Mining - These are the toolsets which are most likely to be missing from the available tools for

an organization. They are complex and usually require an entirely different data structure for optimal performance.

More Audit Notes

Review the tools in terms of how many of each category are available, how well the functions are being performed and user satisfaction. Use the Key Performance Indicators, where applicable. There should be one or two standardized, enterprise supported tools for general use across the organization for such functions as query, reporting and OLAP. There may be a need for more than a single standardized, enterprise supported toolset for these functions, since the tools may vary in performance capabilities. Some, like Cognos, use a proprietary MOLAP (or cube) technology which many users have grown used to and find faster for their summarized and aggregated data. Although, these vendors will claim that all the 'necessary' functions are covered, many users may have special reasons for another toolset. However, if there are more than two in use, analyze the who, what, why factors carefully. Cost and integration factors are especially important to assess. There are, of course, some excellent reasons for the standardization at the enterprise level, including the support and maintenance of the software, as well as the potential for centralized help for the users.

4. Audit Guidelines

The Key Assessment Features have been identified and described in this chapter. As with the rest of the Business Intelligence audit areas, use the relevant Key Performance Indicators (see Chapter 8), where appropriate. We have already identified particular Key Performance Indicators which should be most closely assessed, along with some pointers on particular impact issues. In addition, general audit notes have been included for each of these features. Many of the areas, in fact, most, are specialized and require the assistance and input from the organization information technology specialists. However, the assessment should be based, also, on identifying how these specialists do their jobs and what are their tools for monitoring, review and correction, as much as on the actual functionalities of the hardware, middleware, DBMS, and other Technical Infrastructure.

12-C Business Intelligence Technical Infrastructure

Key Assessment Features	KEY PERFORMANCE INDICATORS													
Rate each Key Assessment Feature for each of the KPI's. Rating should be 1 to 5, with 5 as hightest rating. See the appropriate chapter for audit and rating guidelines	Mngment	Support	BUSINESS ALIGNMENT	PARTNER SHip	Business Goals	Scalability	INTEGRATION	ADAPT ADABILITY	PERFORMANCE	USER FRIENDLY	COMPREHENSION	QUALITY		
Architecture														
Hardware														
Networks														
Middleware														
Database Management Systems														
Meta Data Mgt Systems														
Tools														
Security														
Technical Infrastructure														

Key Assessment Features.

Carefully review the materials in Chapters 3, 4, 5 and 8 prior to beginning the assessment of the Technical Infrastructure. Chapter 3 defines the Capability Maturity Model, Chapters 3 and 4 describe the audit process and tools and guidelines. Chapter 8 identifies and describes the Key Performance Indicators.

The audit and assessment notes are included in the sections on the Key Assessment Features and these should be carefully reviewed and followed during the audit process. This should include an assessment of each Key Assessment Feature, as well as, how well all the features of the Technical Infrastructure work together. This should include a review of the requirements for a sound, integrated and comprehensive Data Integration Platform and Analytics Platform.

Each of the Key Assessment Features of the Business Intelligence Asset Base should be assessed by how well it matches the Business Intelligence and specific platform requirements for the organization. The Key Performance Indicators from Chapter 8 should guide the auditor in the review.

Some of these Key Performance Indicators which are of particular importance in the assessment of the Technical Infrastructure, are:

    · Performance - do the Business Intelligence users get their information as rapidly and in the formats, as needed
    · Scalability - can we add data and users to the system easily and quickly
    · Integration - Is there a common, unified, integrated view of the data and the resulting information, i.e. 'single source of truth'?
    · Efficiency - economy - Is there a common set of resources and infrastructure which reduces the costs and maintainability of the Business Intelligence Technical Infrastructure

A few other audit considerations: Are the software components chosen to provide for the general Business Intelligence requirements and also to meet the specific needs of the organization --- e.g. data modeling tools which will enable normalized and dimensional modeling; extract, transform and load (ETL) tools; user access tools, like Business Intelligence reporting and data mining, forecasting.

We cannot emphasize enough the importance of scalability and adaptability for the Technical Infrastructure. The rapid and frequently unplanned growth and changes in number of users and volumes of data can rupture the fabric of the platforms, if they are not built with flexibility and scalability in mind.

For the **over all rating of the Technical Infrastructure -**
· Level 1 or 0 - Rate the organization at Level 0 or 1, if there is no Data Integration Platform and associated enterprise supported infrastructure. This would mean usually that there are Data Marts scattered around the orga-nization - in use by specific groups.
• Level 5 - Rate the organization at Level 5 only if all the Features can be rated comfortably at a Level 5. Level 4 is a good, competent, mature rating for an organization for infrastructures. If there is also support and infrastructure capabilities for unstructured data, for an enterprise portal (essentially not usually just for Business Intelligence) and specialized web and portal based search facilities - then consider the Level 5 rating.

13

nonTechnical Infrastructure

Chapter Contents

1. Introduction

The nonTechnical infrastructure is made up of all those constructs and features which are not tangible (unlike hardware), but which provide a framework for consistency, integration and seamless, efficient operations within the Business Intelligence Asset Base. This framework must cover all the Business Intelligence assets and ensure a comprehensive cross organization infrastructure.

Because of the cross organization nature of the nonTechnical infra-structure, auditors should look for management and support teams, for particular in-frastructure areas, which are composed of both business and information technology groups. These groups will also, most likely, have membership from various functional arenas, de-pending on the topic for management.

2. The Audit Wheel

The Key Assessment Features for the nonTechnical Infrastructure have been identified and are in included in the Audit Wheel (Fig-ure 13-A). Auditing the nonTechnical Infrastructure component of the Business Intelligence Asset Base should include an assessment of each one of these Key Assessment Features and an overall assess

13-A

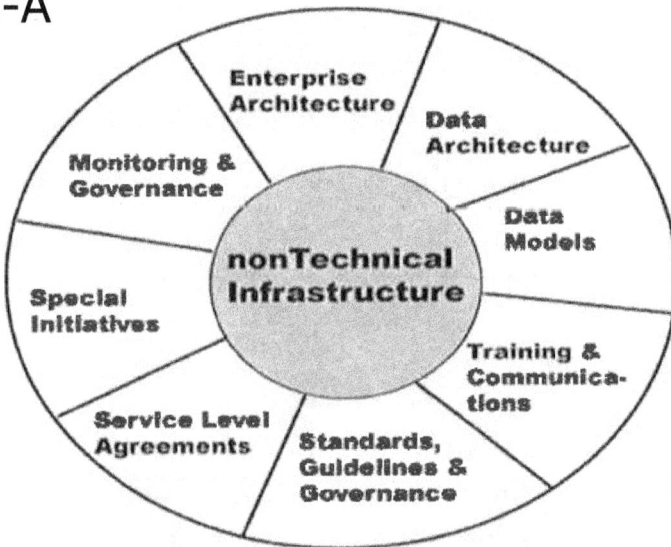

ment of the nonTechnical Infrastructure component of the Business Intelligence Asset Base. The materials in this chapter should provide an understanding of the features and the basic descriptions.

3. Key Assessment Features

3.1 Enterprise Architecture

The organization should have a well planned and documented Enterprise Architecture. The architecture of the Business Intelligence Asset Base should be closely integrated with this Enterprise Architecture. The Enterprise Architecture is described in Chapter 9, The Data Integration Platform. Parts of that discussion will be summarized here for the purposes of describing the relationship and relevance to the nonTechnical Infrastructure. The term `Enterprise Architecture' may have two distinct definitions:

A.   *Enterprise Architecture* may refer to the physical structures and constructs of the organization. This refers to the whole of the organization information technology infrastructure. For example, the organization may have adopted concepts and structures which are Service Oriented Architecture in nature.

B.   *Enterprise Architecture* can also refer to a set of models, constructs and documents which management has developed as a blueprint to guide the organization.

The definition of most relevance for the nonTechnical Infrastructure is the second. Thus, the Enterprise Architecture is defined as a set of documents and plans which have been created by business and information technology members, jointly, to define, map and describe the structures, data and applications - both transactional and business information management - for the organization.

There should be a set of current 'maps', as well as planning documents. This Enterprise Architecture should be widely available, e.g.. on an easily accessible Enterprise Portal. There should be well documented and recognized ownership, stewardship and accepted responsibility for the models, application and data inventories, documentation and communication of contents. This should not be an Information Technology responsibility. The business community should be at least jointly responsible and should retain 'owner-ship'. The development and existence of this Enterprise Architecture is an important base for Business Intelligence creation and management. The presence of such an Enterprise Architecture is itself an indication of management support. The Enterprise Architecture indicates that there has been some planning, groundwork and growth in forging necessary ties between the information technology groups and the business arena.

The value of joint efforts in the creation and maintenance of such an Enterprise Architecture to the organization is important. However, the value of the content of the Enterprise Architecture is equally crucial. Just one example of the critical nature of this work is to provide a base for data integration for Business Intelligence. Data Integration efforts and success can be tied directly to the Enterprise and Data Architecture and the associated data models.

An Enterprise Architecture, among other things, is a blueprint of the operations and business information management systems for the organization. It should include:

- organization plans and structures
- applications inventory and models (logical data models should be linked to the applications)
- applications list of priorities based on business requirements
- business functions inventory and model
- business processes inventory and model
- enterprise data architecture, including master data and other common data artifacts, e.g. reference data

Each of these components of the *Enterprise Architecture* should include full descriptions and any necessary accompanying documentation. Review and update should be periodic and frequent - since these are the basis for all planning for the information technology of the organization. The Enterprise Architecture is designed, developed and kept updated on a regular basis. Any Business plans for the organization should reference this architecture and any changes to strategic or tactical plans and goals should be integrated into the Enterprise Architecture. For example, there should be a priority list for development of new systems and enhancement of others. This priority list should be modified regularly based on business direction and requirements.

3.2 Data Architecture
3.3 Data Models

The most important aspects of the data architecture and the data models for the nonTechnical Infrastructure perspective can be summarized quickly.

· The Data Architecture should be clearly documented and well planned. There needs to be a unifying overall design. Whatever the form, i.e. tools and documentation, it should be easy to understand and readily available to everyone.

· There should be no ambiguity about how the Data Integration Platform is to be structured. The data integration methods should be clear and well documented. If there are to be a normalized central data storage arena for detailed data with dimensional data marts for summarized and aggregated data, everyone needs to understand and follow that design. If, instead, all the data stores are to be designed as dimensional structures, with an integration which uses a BUS architecture of conformed tables, then that should be a recognized design which is universally followed by all Business Intelligence application developers.

· There should be a clear, well designed set of structures for the data. These designs should reflect the requirements associated with the data. The data warehouse presentation data should be easy to access, and allow for fast data retrieval and user response. The design for the relational data stores should reflect the need to find the information and get it out to the users and software interfaces in the required time frames.

· There should be software and methods which are easy to understand and easy to use which will allow for the design of the data. This means that business users need to be able to understand and be involved in the development process.

Database structures. Two of the primary objectives of the database architecture are:

1. The data needs to be designed and structured to allow for integration of the data.

2. The data in the Presentation Library of the Data Integration Plat-form needs to be easily identified, located and quickly accessible.

What is a Logical Data Model. The logical data models define:

· the data objects in the business activities,

· the business relationships among these data objects,

· data structures, elements, and

· the business rules which govern the data objects.

These data models are used to create the physical databases. The structure of the logical data models, as well as, how they are constructed directly impacts:

· success of data integration,

· database performance - both in the back room and front room activities, and

· joint design efforts - i.e. the normalized models are not business intuitive and easy to understand.

There should be maps and models of both the source data stores as well as the Presentation Library of the Data Integration Platform. Source system data models are essential to the identification and location of source data.

Data models are discussed in more detail in Chapter 9, The Data Integration Platform. There are two primary types of logical data models for relational data within an Enterprise Data Warehouse -

normalized and dimensional. The database structures reflect the pictorial design maps.

Normalized Data Model. A normalized data model is a logical database design for relational tables which separates data into discrete, unique entities. The structure of the data in the normalized data model closely resembles the data as used in the business. With this structure, there is a single table for each data object. Each of these data objects, i.e. relational database tables, are connected to all the other data objects through known associations within the data. Normalization of the data also provides the basis for integration of the data. Normalization involves the rules used for laying out the tables for data. The data is present only once in the model and all the data relationships are built directly into the physical structure of the data. This data structure was developed as an efficient way to collect and update transaction data.

Dimensional Data Model. A dimensional data model is a logical database design which optimizes the data structure to make it easy to use in access and use of the data for management decision support, i.e. easy to access, fast responsive query performance. There are fact tables, which hold the measurements; and dimension tables which describe exactly what is known about those measurements, e.g. products, times, etc., related to the measurement of the transaction in question, say the sale of a grocery item. Because of the structure of the single measurement table to many surrounding dimension tables, this model is often called a star schema. There may be multiple copies of the data attributes (data descriptors), i.e. lots of redundant data. Therefore, dimensional data models are unlike the normalized data model, where there are strict mandates against redundancy of the data.

More Audit Considerations.
Data Platform and Modeling Design Issues. There are two major architecture philosophies for the Data Integration Platform, i.e. the Enterprise Data Warehouse. These have been discussed in more detail in Chapter 8.

Source Data Systems. The audit team should specifically find out if there are logical data models available for the source systems? These are necessary in order to identify, locate and extract the data. These are also necessary for all the preliminary design and testing, including the profiling of the data to ensure content and accuracy before actual implementation of the new Business Intelligence application.

Other Data Modeling Assessment Factors. Some of the other data modeling considerations which need to be addressed and reviewed are:

· Integration features: Are the local Business Process or Department-mental data models tied into an enterprise wide data model? How is this validated? Is the Kimball Bus architecture used which counts on 'conformed' dimensions and facts? If so, how is conformity validated.

· What CASE (Computer Assisted Systems Engineering) tools are being used? Do they allow for all standard modeling features, including normalized and dimensional models and is the physical database automatically derived?

3.4. Training and Communications

Sometimes the importance of training and communications aspects of Business Intelligence are overlooked. The Business Intelligence assets of the organization should be marketed to the whole organization. This is the only way to make sure that these assets are used to obtain the most value from the resources. The central Presentation Library of information contains information which can be of use to everyone in the organization. Even those whose needs are not met by the current data need to be aware of the potential of this invaluable information source. How else will they be able to ask for and define their own requirements - if they do not know what is possible.

There should be special programs for introducing people to the data ware-house and business intelligence functions and capabilities. There should be a full range of classes and training from simple, online introductions to class room and CBT training for full 'power user' analytical functions. The communications, e.g. a website or an enterprise portal, should be widely available and marketed. The training should be both online, with people able to interact from their work station, as well as some formal classes, which are instructor led.

Without these training and communications efforts, the data warehouse and Business Intelligence efforts will remain the parochial interests of only a few. People are usually too intent on doing their 'regular' jobs to find out how they can do things better. It is the job of those 'in charge' of the Business Intelligence arena to market the services. These are services which will improve the overall operations and management of the organization. Auditors: Make sure they are spreading the word -- and giving the needed training and support.

3.5. Standards, Guidelines, and Procedures

What are the standards, guidelines and procedures to be audited? What should be identified and assessed? Some examples are:

- data naming, abbreviations, quality
- data stewardship
- data certification
- development methods
- change control and other issues and operations
- testing
- auditing
- data integration standards and governance
- development and maintenance of logical data models and architecture
- service level agreements
- development and enhancement methods, standards and guidelines (see chapter 16)

In review and assessment of these crucial blocks in the non technical framework for Business Intelligence, we need to look for and consider several factors:

What standards, guidelines and procedures are documented and readily available? How are these communicated? Have they been made an integral part of the Business Intelligence development and operations? What kinds of governance methods and teams are in place? How often do the teams meet and what kinds of decisions do they make? Who are the team members - i.e. what are their roles in the organization and responsiblities within the Business Intelligence arena?

3.6 Service Level Agreements

Service Level Agreements have been included as a Key Assessment Feature in several other Business Intelligence components. It is important to mention these important contracts here because they are part of the glue which fuses and creates the foundation for Business Intelligence. These are agreements between any two parties, usually the user community and those who are responsible for creating and delivering the Business Intelligence. They should be written documents which are treated as formal contracts between the two parties. There should be some form of measurement and management of these contracts. Also, both sides should understand exactly what the commitments and expectations mean in terms of cost and value to the organization. If the users expectations are set too high, no one is happy, including those who are trying to satisfy the commitments. There should be careful and complete dialog prior to setting the expectations and writing of the Service Level Agreement. These contracts may be written at any time, including well after the development process has occurred. However, they work best and are most effective when the expectations and commitments are part of the design and development of the Business Intelligence application process. Regular measurement, reporting and common discussions, including revised expectations and commitments are necessary in order to make the process work.

3.7 Special Initiatives

There are numerous programs which benefit the organization and are not necessarily tied to a single department or function. Look for these and see how well they are accomplishing their mission. In particular, the following two initiatives and programs should be identified and assessed - i.e. are they present? What is being accomplished?

What are the stated objectives?

Master Data Management. This is a program initiative which concentrates on the identification, recognition, management and common use of the data across an organization. Master Data are a set of core data elements, along with all their attributes and hierarchies which are common across the whole of the organization. These Master Data are NOT transaction data - which essentially is data which describes the activities, or transactions, of the business. The Master Data are those core data elements which are used to categorize, aggregate and describe the transaction data, e.g. product, customer, employee, account. These are the Dimension values which populate the Dimensional Data Models. The primary focus of a Master Data Management initiative is the accomplishment of what Ralph Kimball describes as Conformed Dimensions. The ultimate goals are to standardize and effectively manage the common data across the organization.

Some of the objectives and results from an effective Master Data Management coupled with the Kimball Data Warehouse Bus are:

- Data Integration,
- 'Control' data which enables users to have a 'common' understanding of the data,
- Assist in the achievement of timely, accurate, consistent information
- Facilitates referential integrity across the system - which, in turn, supports alignment of information and decision making.

The Master Data Management initiative is, in effect, a 'bottom-up' attempt at creating an integrated enterprise data architecture.

Quality Data Initiative. A Quality Data initiative is the result of a recognition by the organization that consistent, accurate, timely data is key to the organization success. A Quality Data initiative or a quality data management program includes the review, careful monitoring and management of data creation and use within the organization. Some of the key elements of any effective program are:

· data stewardship programs - which assign a responsible party to ensure the accuracy, timeliness and other features of the data;
· data certification programs - which ensure that data will have a core 'source of truth' or a single element (out of multiple source copies) which can be accepted as the 'true, accurate data'. Only this data may be used for use and reporting.
· Common Data Definitions.

3.8 Monitoring and Governance

In every case where there is a rule or standards which have been set in place, then there are reasons for the institution of them. The nature of the business and development arena for Business Intelligence requires that these rules and standards be followed. The audit team should look for some form of monitoring and governance for each and every one. This may be regular reviews, during development, automatic via software or manually performed. The consequences when the rules or standards have been violated should at least lead to enforcement of the standardization. If, for example, a system is to go into production, then it should be well known that it must first pass the reviews.

4. Audit Guidelines

Use the information in this chapter, as well as the Key Performance Indicators as described in Chapter 8. If there is little or no evidence of the Key Assessment Feature, rate it as 0 or 1. Highest level should be 4, with a level 5 rating given only in outstanding circumstances, i.e. auditor is particularly impressed with the comprehensive and/ or creativity of the organization. A rating of '5' for the whole of the non-

Technical Infrastructure requires a rat¬ing of '5' for each of the Key Assessment Features. Overall rating should include all the features and may be an average or some features may be given more weight, depending on subjective or objective reasons.

13-B

Rate each Key Assessment Feature for each of the KPI's. Rating should be 1 to 5, with 5 as highest rating. See the appropriate chapter for audit and rating guidelines	KEY PERFORMANCE INDICATORS																	
	MANGMENT	SUPPORTS	BUSINESS ALIGNMENT	PARTNER	SHIP	BUSINESS	GOALS	SCALABILITY	INTEGRA	TION	ADAPT	ABILITY	PERFORM	ANCE	USER	FRIENDLY	COMPREHENSION	QUALITY	VALUE
Enterprise Architecture																		
Data Architecture																		
Data Models																		
Training and Communications																		
Standards and Guidelines																		
Service Level Agreements																		
Special Intiatives																		
Monitoring and Governance																		
nonTechnical Infrastructure																		

(Left margin label: Key Assessment Features)

Business Intelligence non Technical Infrastructure

14

Data

Chapter Contents

1. Introduction

Quality Data. Quality data is the first, second, third and final ingredient of most importance in Business Intelligence. Accuracy and consistency can only be achieved with the commitment of everyone in the organization. Each person in the organization, at some point, is responsible for entering and/or using data. Accuracy and other quality factors can only be maintained when entry and use is monitored and everyone is constantly and automatically vigilant.

Each person has a part to play in creating and maintaining quality data. In this chapter, we discuss what is involved in creating and managing quality data - with results that are successful and consistent. We discuss how we can assess the results.

Definition. The term, Data, unless otherwise noted, refers to the product of Business Intelligence systems. The 'raw' product of the Business Intelligence systems and infrastructures is data. Data is collected and goes through a comprehensive set of transformations and integration to become the final product - business information and then business intelligence. There are a number of concepts, methods, initiatives, and inherent features of data and business information which are reviewed here.

2. The Audit Wheel

The Key Assessment Features for the DATA component of the Business Intelligence Asset Base have been identified and are included in the Audit Wheel (Figure 14-A). Auditing the DATA component of the Business Intelligence Asset Base should include an assessment of each one of these Key Assessment Features and an overall assessment of DATA within the organization. The materials in this chapter should provide an understanding of the features and the basic descriptions.

14 - A

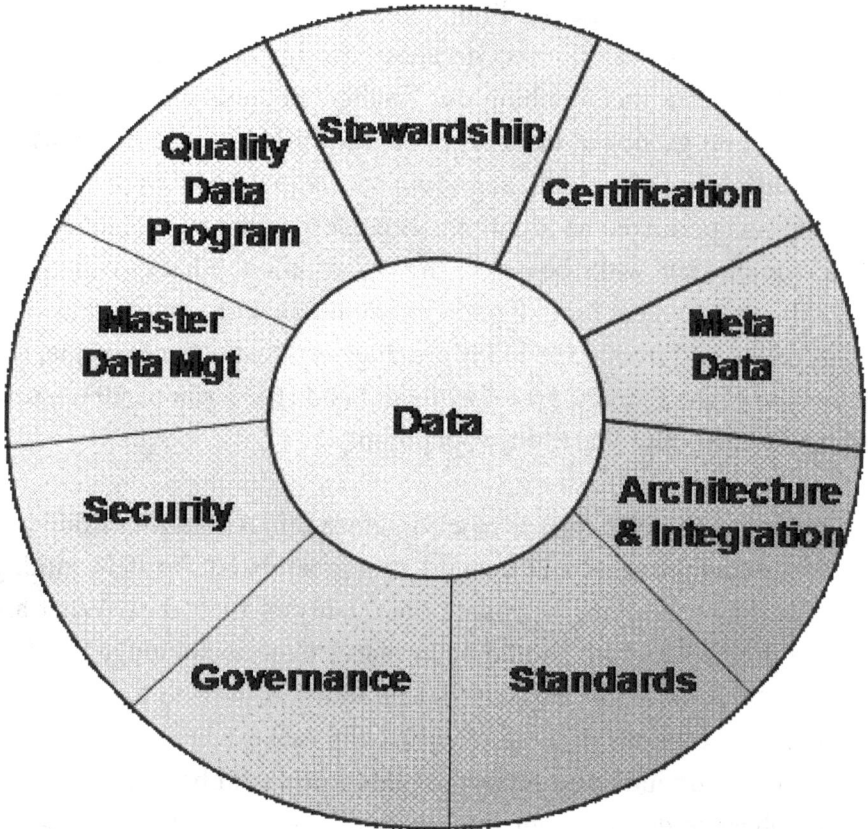

3. Key Assessment Features

3-A Quality Data

What is quality data? Quality Data refers to data that is accurate, that can be easily located and identified, there is only one version of the data, and all the information needed to use the data is readily available.

How does the organization ensure that their data is of the highest quality? Actually, the conditions which have been prevalent in most organizations over the last decades have instead ensured that the available data was anything but 'quality'. Because separate departments and groups of developers created little 'silos' of information for little 'silos' of people using that information. There was no reason that was perceived as important enough for integrating and reconciling the data with the rest of the organization. That has changed. Now, the payment for that parochial style of information technology is due -- and paying the bill is proving very costly. For example, the whole of the Extract, Transform and Load (ETL) can be 60% - 80% of the total Data Warehouse operations.

Assessing the data quality of an organization. Any audit of the data for an organization will depend to a great extent on determining what has been done to ensure the quality of their data. What are the programs which should be in place? How do we judge the data quality? A lot of this also has to do with the answers to the question: Are the programs in place to ensure the data quality? Another major topic for audit and review is: How successful have the Business Intelligence development projects been? A Data Quality Program should be in place and it should be a well recognized effort across the organization.

3.2 Monitor and Governance

Data monitoring requires a consistent policy of review of data to verify that all standards are being met. There should be a zero tolerance acceptance for data errors. This means that, even though there will be errors, each one must be followed up, corrected and any changes to procedures made, if necessary.

Look for documented and embedded activities in development and implementation of Business Intelligence applications for the review of data for compliance with master or common data mandates and all other standards.

Enforcement of Data Quality. Data Quality must be carefully monitored and there should be programs, standards and governance in place to ensure a continuing stream of quality data for the organization. A Data Quality program or initiative within the organization will include some team or group which has responsibility for ensuring operations and governance for at least the programs and internal operations which follow. Before, a Business Intelligence application can go into production, there should be reviews of all of the quality initiatives. For example, this will include data certification, data stewardship, and, of course, the validation of incoming source data, as well as the transformation and integration methods for each piece of data.

Management Support. There should be strong management support for any data quality programs, groups and governance activities. Look for recognition, documentation, and communication to the organization by management of the critical nature for the organization of a 'single source of truth' - i.e. data which has been cleaned, reformatted to meet a common view, reconciled so that there is a single piece of data to meet the common understanding with a common meaning.

3.3 Data Stewardship.

Each group, category and unit of data should be assigned a business owner, directly responsible for the quality of that data. The assignments may be for specific categories and groups. Most often this stewardship will be the responsibility of the associated business departments or business area. This means that the data stewardship is usually assigned to those who have the responsibility for whatever transactions or operational activities are associated with collecting the data. Stewardship requires that the data, as well as all the meta data which should be connected to that data, is validated by those who understand the data best -for organization use. If there is a problem with the accuracy or any aspect of the data, then that data steward is the person to whom questions and repair assignments are directed. There should be a single person, i.e. specific role, not necessarily by name (with backup) with the primary responsibility for specific data. That person should also be responsible for input, update and general documentation and communication of the meta data or information about that data. This should include all the related meta data for the data, including the Enterprise Meta Data Repository, if there is one.

3.4. Data Certification.

This is a program and tagging operation which allows for identifying data which is the original, 'vetted'/ reconciled - the recognized 'single source of truth' . The certification is essentially a mark of approval for the data which is branded somehow (perhaps a unique attribute) - so that everyone will know that they are not getting an unauthorized replication.

Data Profiling. More Data Warehouse and Business Intelligence implementations have failed due to inaccuracies and general junkiness' of the source data than can be counted. The system is architected, designed, fully developed and the first streams of data are no good. Weeks and months are usually spent trying to clean up and reconcile the source data. In many cases, it just cannot be done. The data is hopelessly unusable. The source data may not even contain values which correlate to the fields which are defined in the application documentation. In this case, the integrity and accuracy of the expected data for the Data Warehouse can be completely destroyed. The only answer to this is to include a special set of activities in every Business Intelligence development which is designed to test and profile the source data before any major money and time is spent. If this is a part of the development methodology - there should be full documentation as well as anecdotal evidence of its use and effectiveness. Look for this data profiling pre-development work.

3.5. Master Data Management.

Any organization has a set number of business processes and associated data sets. The master data are the core elements, along with their dimensions, hierarchies, properties, attributes. which are used across the organization. Product and Customer data are just two examples of master or common data for the organization. The master data might consist of the common tables (dimensions) of the Kimball Data Warehouse BUS architecture. Master Data is usually part of a data architecture plan in the Enterprise Architecture. Master Data is not transaction or operational data. (These are activity related and describe the operations of the business.) The Master Data are what the transactions are 'about'. For example, 2 of Product abc were sold across the counter at Joe's grocery store on May 9. What exactly is product abc? Ensuring that these master data are kept standardized, completely the same in format and in common use, with exactly the same data elements and descriptors, is of crucial importance. There should be a cross organization team of both business and information technology specialists who select and govern these master data. This team should be responsible for setting up Change Control mechanisms and enforcing data uniformity and integrity for any new Business Intelligence applications. This might be the same team which is responsible for data stewardship and data certifica-tion programs.

3.6. Architecture and Integration

The internal operations of the Data Warehouse includes sourcing, reformatting, cleansing, and integration of the data. Any audit of the data quality for an organization needs to include a review of the data integration platform and the Business Intelligence Engine. (see chapters 9 and 11)

3.7. Meta Data.

In Chapter 15, meta data was described and the important part meta data plays in the nonTechnical infrastructure for Business Intelligence was highlighted. In data quality, meta data is the prime player. Without information about the data, there is no data to information to intelligence translation. The meta data requirements should be specifically documented and the entry and tag of that meta data should be subject to review and governance activities. Meta data includes anything which describes the data, the history of the data, location, etc. For example, some of the meta data are: table names and allowed values; column names and allowed values; data steward; definitions, business rules, transformation rules, dates and 'who did it' audit information for all changes or movement of the data, including ETL and archival activities. Meta data is not just tied to single data tables and columns, however. There should be meta data which describes the data models and the physical databases. There also should be meta data which describes business processes and activities - essentially any parts of the en-terprise architecture and associated models. If there is no formal enterprise architecture, then there should still be meta data which describes these processes. Where is the meta data kept? There should be clear documentation on exactly where the meta data is contained, how it is associated with the data and who maintains it -- i.e. which is system derived and any which is manually or otherwise, entered.

Common Business Language. An Enterprise Meta Data Repository is an excellent source of integration activities and interface for users. Queries can be expedited when there is a place for users to look up and identify common business identifiers. If this Enterprise Meta Data Repository is interactive this allows an evolution of the business language. This would mean that, not only can the users search for and use the contents of the repository, but they can also create and update the contents. These updates should then be fed back into the systems - e.g. logical data models - and used to update the applications. This kind of interactive Enterprise Meta Data Repository is not common. See what the organization has, anyway. This would be a major plus in their rating.

3.8. Standards

There should be well documented standards for every aspect of data which will impact quality and consistency. This includes everything from naming standards and conventions, abbreviations, formats, meta data requirements, to mapping and input profiling.

A Data Quality Cross Organization team should be in place with responsibility for all those standards and policies and procedures necessary to ensure data quality.

3.9 Monitor and Governance

Data monitoring requires a consistent policy of review of data to verify that all standards are being met. There should be a zero tolerance for data errors. This means that, even though there will be errors, each one must be followed up, corrected and any necessary changes to data as well as to procedures should also be made, if necessary.

Look for documented and embedded activities in development and imple-mentation of Business Intelligence applications for the review of data for compliance with master of common data mandates and all other standards.

4.0 Audit Guidelines

Use the information in this chapter. Review Chapter 8 for the Key Perfor-mance Indicators. If there is little evidence of the target Key Assessment Feature, rate it as 0 or 1. Highest level should be 4, with a level 5 rating given only in outstanding circumstances. A rating of 5 for the whole of the Data component requires a rating 5 for each of the Key Assessment Features. The Overall rating should include all the features and may be an average or some features may be given more weight, depending on auditor judgement.

Rate each Key Assessment Feature for each of the KPI's. Rating should be 1 to 5, with 5 as hightest rating. See the appropriate chapter for audit and rating guidelines	KEY PERFORMANCE INDICATORS															
	MANAGEMENT	SUPPORT	BUSINESS ALIGNMENT	PARTNER SHIP	BUSINESS	GOALS	Scalabil	INTEGRA TION	ADAPT	ABILITY	PERFORANCE	USER	FRIENDLY	COMPREHENSION	QUALITY	VALUE
DATA Quality Program																
Data Stewardship																
Data Certification																
Meta Data																
Data Architecture & Integration																
, Standardss																
Governance & Security																
Master Data Management																
DATA																

Key Assessment Features

Meta Data

Chapter Contents

1. Introduction

Meta data is information about data. Meta data may be combined with raw data to transform it into information. We need to be able to see it, access it, use it and change it, at any time, in a fast, easy manner. The current state of meta data architecture and technology does not allow an organization to easily provide for visibility, communications and accessibility across the Business Intelligence Asset-Base. Meta data points of collection are usually the toolsets within the Business Intelligence Asset Base, e.g. ETL and data modeling.

There is no unified, central architecture. Any unification comes from customized applications. There are several vendor developed Enterprise Meta Data Repositories which provide some functionality for accessibility and a meta data map.

2. The Audit Wheel

15 - A

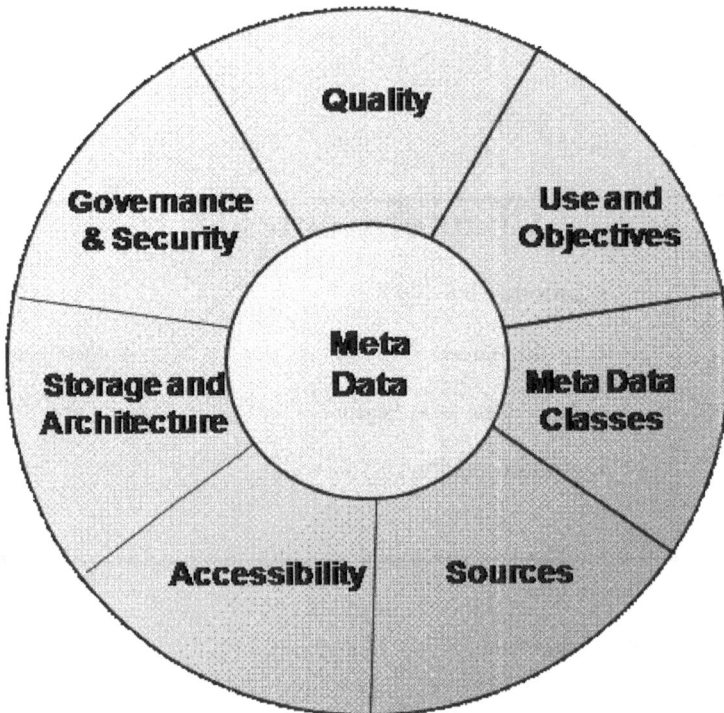

Meta Data

Quality

Use and Objectives

Meta Data Classes

Sources

Accessibility

Storage and Architecture

Governance & Security

The Key Assessment Features for Meta data are identified in the audit wheel in Figure 15-A. These Key Assessment Features will drive the audit and review of the meta data creation and use within the organization. The remainder of this chapter describes the features in more detail.

3. Key Assessment Features

3.1 Quality

Meta data quality refers to the following aspects of the meta data:
- Complete, i.e. comprehension. Has all the meta data which is required to understand and use the data been collected and made accessible and available.
- Accuracy -- is it accurate and up to date.
- Timeliness - is it available when needed
- Format - is the format usable?
- Accessible - can anyone with the need and proper secu¬rity get to the meta data.
- Uniform and integrated -- is the meta data consistent across the enterprise data stores.

3.2 Use and Objectives

Data Description. Meta data describes the data. What is it? What are the exact meanings? Where did it come from? Meta data traces the exact path of DATA across the organization infrastructures and stores. It describes and traces the business history. Meta data identifies the exact location (s) of the data.

Common Business Language. Meta data also creates a common business language for the organization. Everyone should be able to use the meta data library as a source for definitions and data descriptions for words in use in the organization.

Audit, Administration, Security. Meta data provides the audit and administration information for the data, e.g. who is the data steward? who created the data? how do we know that the data is certified?

Impact Analysis . The meta data should be an excellent guide to allow changes in the data bases. Where is all the data which will be impacted by any change? However, meta data also needs to be changed, at times. A major requirement for impact analysis is that each and every piece of data and meta data must be quickly identifiable, locatable, and accessible, across the whole of the Business Intelligence Asset Base. All relationships must be equally identifiable and accessible.

3.3 Meta Data Classes

Meta data may be described more fully by defining the type and uses. A major classification method which is useful in understanding more about meta data are the categories of Business and Technical Meta Data.

Business Meta Data

Business meta data is developed in cooperation with and used most extensively by organization members outside information technology. Much of this business meta data has a similar content as technical meta data - since there is a need for names, descriptions and locations of data for both. However, there is additional information required by the business community. Data derivations, timing and various alias and other descriptive and associated information, including graphics, might be important to the business user. This meta data also includes all those components required to query, research and report against the data warehouse data. The structure and presentation of this business meta data is developed to meet the business requirements and includes at least subject and function hierarchies. Some of the types of uses are for:

1. Query and Analysis
2. Standard Reporting
3. Common Business Language
4. Management special needs.

Technical Meta Data

Technical Meta Data is used by the applications and by information technology professionals and business power users in extracting and processing data. Technical meta data describes the physical properties and locations of the data elements - i.e. databases, formats, names of rows, tables, descriptions, formats. Technical meta data also includes information about how the data is sourced and moved about the organization structures, stores and systems. It is important to be able to trace the origins and movements of the data across the Business Intelligence Asset Base and history.

3.4 Meta Data Sources

Meta data comes into the Business Intelligence Asset Base from various entry points. Some of the sources are:
- Applications, including reports and source data stores and

data maps and models
- Business Intelligence Tools
- Design and development of new Business Intelligence Applications, including from data models, data collection and design
- Data Base Management Systems, which collect and distribute technical meta data
- Data Dictionaries
- Audit, scheduling and operations tools and processes
- ETL tools and processes
- Data Mining tools
- Data Profiling
- Enterprise Meta Data Repositories
- Direct entry into Enterprise Data Repositories

3.5 Meta Data Accessibility

There are several key points to make about Meta Data accessibility. Accessibility means locating data and meta data wherever it is in the Business Intelligence Asset Base. Accessibility means locating each and every related piece of data and meta data and providing relevant relationships among them. Accessibility requirements are dictated by the requirements and objectives for the data and the meta data.

1. Cross organization access and use. Impact Analysis requires the capability of identifying and locating each piece of data, whatever the toolset or location. If we make changes to data or meta data, there is a need to access all related data and meta data across the system. We need to be able to identify and locate every piece of associated data and meta data.

2. Common Business Language - Everyone in the organiza-tion must have the same understanding of business

terms and must be using the same business terms in reference to specific data. All should have access and should be able to update and create new meta data. This allows for the growth and evolution of the meta data into a quality foundation for a common business language.

3.   Audit and history of data and meta data - There is a need to know who created the data and meta data, and statistics about the movement and change. If something is wrong (or right) or needs follow-up - then this meta data becomes a crucial factor. Sometimes even the success of the organization may rest on tracing specific data and meta data.

4. Understand the data. Complete descriptions and definitions of data . We need complete information about names, definitions, and how the data is used in order to understand the data.

3.6 Storage and Architecture

Meta data architecture may be one of the most important leading indicators of how well an organization is handling the creation and management of Business Intelligence Assets. There are, for practical purposes, several different architectures which may apply to the organization meta data storage. Customization by the organization is the primary way that any upgrades to meta data architecture can be made at the current state of the technology base.

A basic architecture is the one which naturally occurs by the collection and use of various tools which collect meta data. The meta data is collected and retained in various tools used across the organization - i.e. ETL, CASE, DBMS.

This elementary level of meta data architecture may be all that the organization has in place. The organization has essentially no real meta data plan. There is no communication or bridges across the tools except what has been included in the original toolsets. No way to provide for impact analysis or sharing of common language and movement of technical and audit data through the Business Intelligence Asset Base. This type of meta data architecture should be considered as a Level 1 maturity level.

There are a number of other levels and types of meta data libraries which satisfy to a certain extent the primary objectives. At a high level of maturity, one of the possible architectures would be a Data Warehouse for meta data. There might also be some form of centralized meta data repository and a full set of bridges, channels, and access and search methods which tie all the meta data together across the Business Intelligence Asset Base. (See Section 4 on Auditing)

The objectives for a mature architecture for meta data for the Business Intelligence Asset Base include the following:
- Full integration of the meta data with full warehouse-like capabilities for identification, location, access and use.
- Full accessibility to all the meta data across the Business Intelligence Asset Base, with bridges or a centralized integrated storage library.
- Research, search, and manipulation of meta data, as data values.
- Use of a standard meta model and mapping process for design and development.
- Supports existing meta data in existing tools and allows for creation and update through the tools sets or through the Meta

Data warehouse toolsets.

· Portals and universal access from across the enterprise, with creation and update capabilities and reverse direction update into the toolsets as well as the meta data central repository (or meta data warehouse).

· Automated processes for maintaining meta data from collection points and streaming data or other methods for updating meta data central data repository or meta data warehouse.

3.7. Governance and Security

How are security for meta data and for data different? The fields and values for the meta data may be sensitive and, depending on the organization, may be proprietary. In all cases, the meta data will give any competitor a good approximation of what the company data is and where it is located. Therefore, it is most sensible to treat the meta data as a special form of data values. The security demanded by the organization for their data may apply to meta data. The organization must make this determination. For auditing purposes, review each of the toolsets or points of collection for the meta data and find out exactly what security precautions are taken. The accessibility through user interfaces, e.g. portals, and meta data repositories should be explored.

4.0 Audit Guidelines

The list of objectives and highest level potential for capabilities for a meta data system and architecture which has been described in this chapter, is simply a wish list for what might happen in the future. Because of the current state of technology, most organizations are closer to Level 1 than Level 5. However, the auditor should look for some visible sign that organization management has recognized the needs for access to meta data across the Business Intelligence Asset Base. Designers and management should be exploring a next step in the technological evolution of meta data architectures. Auditors should carefully review comprehension and quality of the meta data being collected. How much is collected, what kinds, how is it accessed, how is it used? Can the meta data be accessed quickly; How much is visible? and is it possible to use the meta data for impact analysis? This means, if there is a need to change something, do we know everywhere the change needs to be made? The auditor should find that meta data is being collected from all the major sources and that there is meta data to satisfy all the major functions required for meta data - e.g. audit, administration, history and tracking, business definitions and descriptions, technical meta data, including locations, formats, and stewards and certification information.

Audit of Architecture and Meta Data Systems

Industry environment and practices today have not evolved to the point of a common industry recognition of the need for a centralized meta data management system. Meta data is embedded in multiple tools sets, from ETL drivers to CASE tools. Meta data is incorporated and plays a major role in the services objects in Service Oriented Architectures. In fact, the use of meta data is common.

15 - B

| Key Assessment Features | KEY PERFORMANCE INDICATORS | | | | | | | | | | | | | |
Rate each Key Assessment Feature for each of the KPI's. Rating should be 1 to 5, with 5 as highest rating. See the appropriate chapter for audit and rating guidelines	Mangement	Support	BUSINESS ALGNMNT	PARTNER SHIP	Business Goals	Scalabii	INTEGRATION	ADAPT	ABiLiTY	PERFORM ANCE	USER FRIENDLY	COMPRE HENSION	QUALITY	VALUE
Quality														
Use & Objectives														
Classes														
Sources														
Accessibility														
, Architecture														
Governance & Security														
META DATA														

In assessing the organization meta data resources, the audit team should research and evaluate based on the following criteria:

· Level 1: The organization meta data is limited to that which is embedded in the toolsets and various services and applications requirements.

· Level 2: There is some mechanism for interfacing the meta data among some of the various tools and applications.

· Level 3: There is a mechanism for making the meta data visible, and accessing and using any of the meta data in the Business Intelligence Asset Base.

· Level 4: There is a strong connectivity among all the points, or nodes, which contain meta data. All the meta data in the system is 'visible' and can be accessed. The access is universal and users can see and use the meta data through search engines or similar toolsets.

· Level 5: A strong, centralized meta data library exists which allows for interconnectivity and visibility of all meta data in the system. This library includes a creation, update and management system which allows users and developers to access and update the meta data. There is universal access to the meta data and the management system. In addition, there is a strong, monitored and well managed system for creation and governance of technical and business meta data. This includes the development and support for a business language repository.

16

Development Methodology

Chapter Contents

1. Introduction

2. Audit Wheel

3. Key Assessment Features

4. Audit Guidelines

1. Introduction

The way that the applications are designed and developed is critical to the success of Business Intelligence in an organization. There should be well documented and communicated methods and processes for development of Business Intelligence applications. There should be a program which defines the development process - step by step. The process can be complex.

The Information Base which is the subject of any new business intelligence development project is, most often, an active, existing library. Development methods need to be consistent and should incorporate safeguards for the current information. There are numerous other requirements which should be incorporated into the development process in order to meet the organization needs for a continuing base of quality Business Intelligence. An important first step is to ensure the application team understands the complexities of the Business Intelligence Asset Base for the organization.

The purpose of this chapter is not to define the development process. However, there are a number of principles and constructs which we need to ensure are present, i.e. included in the methodology, in order to provide for and protect the quality of Business Intelligence assets. Any audit of the Business Intelligence assets for the organization requires a close review of the existing development process. This chapter will define some of the more critical points which should be analyzed.

2. The Audit Wheel

Any audit should begin with the question of whether there is a documented set of processes for Business Intelligence design and development. There are some guidelines which should be recognized by the development teams and the management of the organization. These should be documented somewhere or there should be answers for each item if put in the form of a question to the project managers and sponsors. Some of the '50,000 foot level type of observations' are noted here. Most of these are described in the Key Performance Indicators (Chapter 8).

Is the project aligned to business goals?

Does it have complete management support? What are the manage-ment expectations? What are the organization impacts and political ramifications?

Is there joint business and IT management and participation?

Are we building in flexibility and adaptability into the application?

The rest of the chapter is devoted to ground level observations and integral features for a Business Intelligence development project.

16 - A

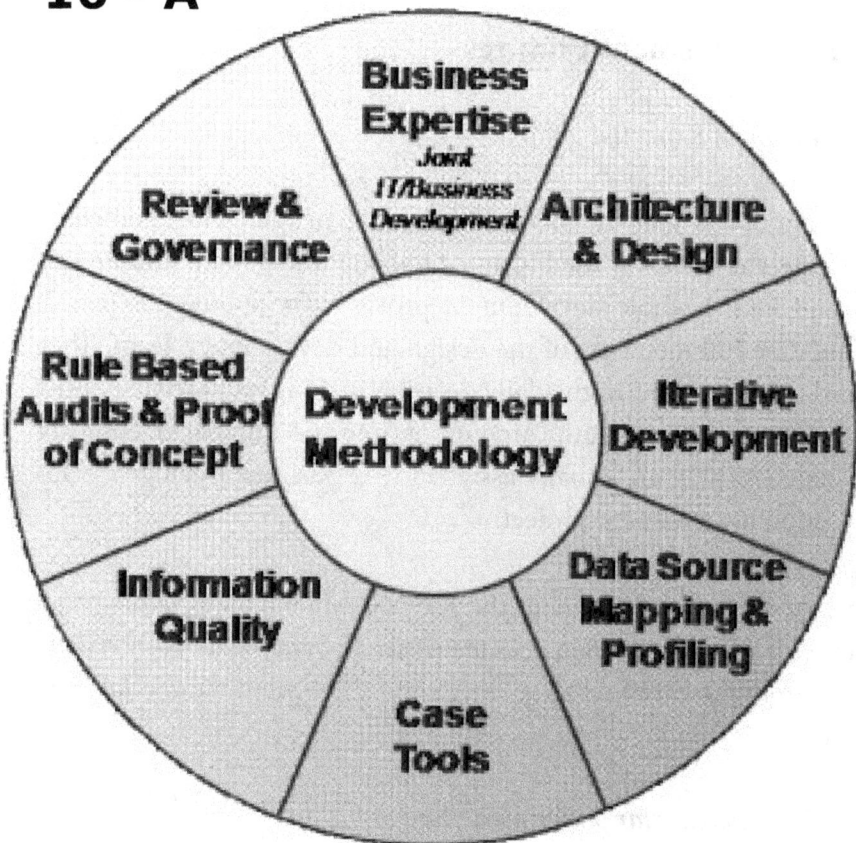

Business Expertise — Joint IT/Business Development

Architecture & Design

Review & Governance

Rule Based Audits & Proof of Concept

Development Methodology

Iterative Development

Information Quality

Data Source Mapping & Profiling

Case Tools

The Key Assessment Features for a Business Intelligence development methodology have been identified and are included in the Audit Wheel (Figure 16-A). Auditing the Development Methodology component of the Business Intelligence Asset Base should include an assessment of each one of these Key Assessment Features, plus an overall assessment of the Development Methodology component of the Business Intelligence Asset Base. The materials in this chapter should provide an understanding of the features and the basic descriptions.

3. Key Assessment Features

3.1. Business Expertise

It is important that the business users (i.e. people who understand and use the business intelligence product) understand and are involved in the whole development process. These business people should be full members of the design and development team. They need to be involved in the daily decision making and activities. Any audit should check out the amount of time and number of end user resources which are usually assigned to a Business Intelligence application development project.

One of the major benefits of the Kimball philosophy of Data Warehouse architecture is that it seems easier to involve the business/end users from the initial stages of design and throughout the development process.

The inherent star pattern structure of the dimensional model par-

allels the user requirements and optimizes the process of accessing and using the information. The primary alternative to the dimensional model is the normalized data model, which is architected to reflect the organization structure and to optimize the creation and update of the transaction data. The design and development of a normalized relational database requires database experts. It is not so easy for the business user to understand the design and process.

In auditing the Business Intelligence Development process, take a look at who is assigned to the projects (i.e. roles and organization job responsibilities), what kinds of teams are formed, and how many specialists like the business experts and data architects, modelers and ETL specialists are available. Lack of resources certainly can impact the development success rate.

Management Support. The need for management support is so pervasive and well recognized that it is commonly written into any planning documentation. The need for management support for the Business Intelligence application development process is just as important.

3.2. Architecture and Design

The integration of data is of primary importance in building a successful Enterprise Data Warehouse. A well established, uniform architecture is one of the primary constructs. The architecture should include such features as incorporation of master data and quality data precepts. There should be review and governance to ensure that the architecture patterns and rules are upheld.

The primary architecture models for the Enterprise Data Warehouse have been discussed in previous chapters. The important considerations in the audit of the Business Intelligence development methodology are:

- Has an architecture been clearly defined for the Enterprise Data Warehouse?
- Is there a strong conceptual understanding of that architecture and the designs and processes required to create a consistent infrastructure using the architecture concepts?
- Is the architecture used as the pattern for design and development in a consistent manner?

The two most prominent architectures and philosophies for the design of an Enterprise Data Warehouse are those presented by Inmon and by Kimball. The auditor should research how well and how consistently the organization developers adhere to the required methods for the chosen architecture.

Disagreement and ambiguity about the architecture foundation of the Enterprise Data Warehouse are not unusual and can be devastating to the integrity of the data warehouse library(s).

3.3. Iterative Development

The Big Bang theory of Data Warehouse development has been proven to create a big history of failures. Iterative design and development provides for the design and development of small pieces of an application at a time. Since there are fewer and less complex parts to go wrong or be misunderstand, this approach allows an easier management process. This iterative development concept is also know as the 'don't bite off more than you can chew' philosophy. Both business and information technology people can easily visualize the design. Everyone sees the results faster. They can see and use and change, as necessary, the resulting information faster, in more easily understood small 'chunks', and in a more informal, less stressful, manner. The information can be made to conform to the real needs of the business user, as those needs are recognized. The final results are more likely to fit the exact requirements and the overall costs should be much lower. These are just a few of the reasons for the recognition by the industry that iterative development of applications is the most successful approach.

There are a number of formal development methodologies available on the market today. The auditor should identify any in use within the organization and explore the following questions: Do the developers understand and use the formal methodology? How well does it work for them? Are the results consistent and successful? Ask the developers and look at the documentation and some of the development project documentation and results.

3.3. Data Profiling

Sampling the source data and ensuring that it is as defined in the documentation and data models is important to success. The source data may not be as documented, may not have integrity and/or may not be accurate and up to date. It is best to find this out well before the development work begins. Any changes to the source data needs to be recognized and dealt with as soon as possible in the Business Application project. The data sampling should be done early, before a lot of costs have been sunk into the project. If there is just no way to obtain data with integrity and accuracy - i.e. if the data source is corrupted and unfixable - then the project should be abandoned until the data can be found or created. This is a hard lesson and almost never learned without some rough experience.

3.4. Source Mapping

As part of the design process, the Business Intelligence data requirements are identified. Exact locations of the data, formats, how to extract them --these are all key parts of the Business Intelligence application design. The auditor should make sure that the development documentation includes the requirement for maps which pinpoint the source data. There should also be a requirement and descriptions of all the documentation which is needed for the source data. This should include business meta data, e.g. definitions, as well as technical meta data, including, for example, formats and database structures.

The data profiling should match the data values found against the expecta-tions based on the documentation. The design and development of the extraction process requires that the source data be mapped and matched with the target data.

In addition to the data source maps, there should be documentation and identification of available meta data.

3.5. Case Tools

Automated, easy to use and to understand software (CASE - Computer Assisted Software Engineering) should be available for each of the design and development steps and functions. This includes, for example, the design of the logical data models and the design, development and runtime processing of the Extract, Transform and Load processing. In addition, it is just as important that there are team members who understand the information requirements, the development process, and how to use the CASE tools.

In the audit process, look for CASE tools which are well established and are being used within the organization. Check that these tools meet industry standards. This usually means a review of the web site and technical descriptive literature. Also, check with the developers. How well are the tools accepted. Do they like the tool and why. Are there any specific issues and how critical are they?

3.6. Prototypes and Rule Based Audits

There is a significant amount of risk associated with any Business Intelligence application development project. Some of this risk comes from unknown factors in the source data and the source applications. We have discussed activities to mitigate some of these risks, i.e. data mapping and data profiling. There are some other major methods which the organization should be using as standard practice. With a little research, the auditor should be able to determine whether these are a part of the project development methodology. The practices should be well documented and understood by any of the project teams. The following practices should be included in the standard development process:

- Rule based Audits allow for testing of sample source data. (Data profiling is also an up front testing of source data - but differs slightly in that it is checking the validity and accuracy of the data.) This allows the determination that source data along with the known business rules would allow the creation of the desired target data.
- A Proof of Concept or pilot/test with a set of data which is considerably smaller than the final production data volumes can also assist in reducing the risk for the whole project.

3.7. Information Quality

All the requirements which are necessary for data quality must be built in - during the development process. There should be parts of the formal or informal Development Methodology which specifically addresses the data quality issues. This should include comprehensive meta data. In addition, during design and development process, data stewards should be identified and assigned the responsibility for specific meta data and data. The project documentation should include the identification of these data stewards. There should also be some method for certification of data and other data quality constructs which enforce the integrity and accuracy of the data. These features should be integral to the development process.

Auditors should look for specific documentation related to incorporation of data quality into the design and development process. There should also be some indication that these are included in the governance and review process.

3.8. Review and Governance

Application development projects should have consistent and regular reviews at various points in the process. The reviews should include resources external to the development team. There should be a documented review process. The contents should include review of all the audit points, including, for example, follow-up on information quality, profiling, and mapping results.

4.0 Audit Guidelines

Use the information in this chapter, as well as the Key Performance Indicators as described in Chapter 8. If there is little or no evidence of the Key Assessment Feature, rate it as 0 or 1. Highest level should be 4, with a level 5 rating given only in outstanding circumstances. This might mean, for example, that the auditor is particularly impressed with the comprehensive and/ or creativity of the organization. A rating of '5' for the whole of the Development Methodology component requires a rating of '5' for each of the Key Assessment Features. The Overall rating should include all the features and may be an average. However, some features may be given more weight, depending on subjective or objective reasons by the auditor.

16-B

Key Assessment Features / Rate each Key Assessment Feature for each of the KPI's. Rating should be 1 to 5, with 5 as hightest rating. See the appropriate chapter for audit and rating guidelines	Management	Supports	BUSINESS	ALIGNMENT	PARTNERSHIP	Business	Goals	Scalability	INTEGRATION	ADAPT	AB PLTFORM	PERFORMANCE	USER	FRIENDLY	COMPREHENSION	QUALITY	VALUE
Business Expertise & Resource Utilization																	
Design & Architecture																	
Iterative Development																	
Data Source Mapg & Profilg																	
CASE Tools																	
Rule Based Audits & Proof/concept																	
Information Quality																	
Review & Governance																	
Development Methodology																	

www.ingramcontent.com/pod-product-compliance
Lightning Source LLC
Chambersburg PA
CBHW060340220326
41598CB00023B/2767